THE
HALOGEN
OVEN
COOKBOOK

Maryanne Madden

hamlyn

An Hachette UK Company
www.hachette.co.uk

First published in Great Britain in 2010 by
Hamlyn, a division of Octopus Publishing
Group Ltd
Endeavour House
189 Shaftesbury Avenue
London
WC2H 8JY
www.octopusbooks.co.uk

Maryanne Madden asserts the moral right to
be identified as the author of this work.

ISBN 978-0-600-62177-5

A CIP catalogue record for this book is
available from the British Library.

Printed and bound by CPI Group
(UK) Ltd, Croydon, CR0 4YY

10 9 8 7 6

Read your halogen oven manual before you
begin and preheat the halogen oven if
required according to the manufacturer's
instructions. Because halogen ovens vary
slightly from manufacturer to manufacturer,
check recipe timings with the manufacturer's
directions for a recipe using the same
ingredients. All recipes for this book were
tested in a Pro Cooks Halogen Oven.

Standard level spoon measures are used in all
recipes:
1 tablespoon = one 15 ml spoon
1 teaspoon = one 5 ml spoon

Both metric and imperial measurements are
given for the recipes. Use one set of measures
only, not a mixture of both.

Medium eggs have been used throughout.

Fresh herbs should be used unless otherwise
stated.

A few recipes contain nuts and nut
derivatives. Anyone with a known nut allergy
must avoid these.

This book contains some dishes made with
raw or lightly cooked eggs. It is prudent for
more vulnerable people such as pregnant and
nursing mothers, invalids, the elderly, babies
and young children to avoid raw or lightly
cooked eggs.

contents

introduction

Halogen ovens use innovative halogen technology to cook almost any type of food. These compact table-top cookers are convenient and easy to use, and they are generally much quicker than a conventional oven. The tiered racks make it possible to cook food quickly and allow fat to drain away, making the food prepared by this relatively new way of cooking both tasty and healthy.

This cookbook contains over 100 recipes to cook in your halogen oven. The dishes range from basic roast meat recipes to help you get started with your oven to more complicated fish and vegetable dishes and desserts and bakes. The instructions are easy to follow and provide you with a wide variety of ways to use your halogen oven, whether you are cooking for the whole family or making a quick lunch to eat alone or enjoy with friends.

all about halogen ovens

Halogen ovens work by means of an infrared halogen element that is sited in the lid. This heats up almost instantly, so you will find that your halogen oven is more cost-efficient than a conventional cooker because you do not have to preheat it. In addition, most cooking times are about 40 per cent less than in an ordinary oven, again saving money. Moreover, the fan-assisted air circulation cooks food evenly, meaning that it is usually unnecessary to turn items.

You can use your halogen oven to bake, roast, steam and grill food, and some models also have a thaw function, allowing you to cook frozen foods without waiting for them to defrost.

Unlike a microwave oven, a halogen oven will brown food just like a conventional oven, making it easy to prepare succulent roast meats, such as chicken and pork, with crisp, crunchy skin and crackling.

The arrangement of racks within the halogen oven means that there is ample room to cook a whole meal for your family, including plenty of vegetables, or a simple small meal for one person, and once you have got used to using your oven you will find that it is versatile, economical and much easier to clean than a conventional oven.

halogen oven basics

Most ovens are supplied with:

- Base stand and housing
- Glass bowl
- Removable glass lid with halogen element and electrical lead
- Steel racks
- Steel handles so that you can safely move the racks and other containers.

The glass bowl is usually 30–33 cm (12–13 inches) wide and about 18 cm (7 inches deep).

When you are using your halogen oven it's important that you make full use of all accessories that are supplied. Most models are equipped with two cooking racks – an upper and a lower one – which can be used alone or in combination to increase the number of dishes you can cook at the same time. Because the racks raise the food from the base of the oven, the food will be cooked more quickly than if it is sitting directly in the base of the bowl. Although you won't damage the bowl by placing food in it, it will take longer to cook.

self-cleaning function

The glass bowl can be easily washed in hot soapy water or in your dishwasher, but if you are buying a new halogen oven it's worth looking for one with a self-cleaning function, which you can use as follows:

- Half-fill the glass bowl with hot water
- Push down the handle to lock it
- Turn the setting to the wash function
- Set the timer to the required time (usually 10–15 minutes).

Never immerse the lid in water. After use, keep it clean by wiping it with a damp cloth.

other equipment

You can use all the utensils, baking sheets and casserole dishes that you would use in your conventional oven in your halogen oven, and, unlike in your microwave oven, you can safely use metal dishes and baking tins.

casserole dish

For most of the recipes in this book you will need a casserole dish holding about 2.5 litres (4 pints). You will sometimes need a smaller dish and, occasionally, a larger one, so always check before you begin that your casserole dish will fit inside the glass bowl and that you can easily lift it out and into the bowl. A casserole dish that is about 23 cm (9 inches) across will be ideal.

Although it's possible to cook food directly in the bowl, cooking in a casserole dish that you can place on the lower rack allows the hot air to circulate around the food, cooking it more quickly and more evenly.

baking sheets

Some manufacturers supply baking sheets and roasting tins specifically for use in their halogen ovens. Round ones are especially useful and are available on the Internet. However, if you cannot find an appropriately sized baking sheet you can always cover one of the racks with kitchen foil.

kitchen foil

Many of the recipes in this book recommend that you use foil to protect food from burning or over-browning on top. This is because the halogen oven operates in a similar way to a grill – it will cook food on the outside more quickly than the inside – so you should cover food with foil to make sure the top doesn't burn.

If your casserole dish has a snugly fitting lid you can use the lid to cover a dish, but often the lid makes a casserole dish heavy and awkward to lift, especially when you are wearing oven gloves, whereas foil is light and easy to use.

getting started

To set up your halogen oven place the metal housing on a secure, perfectly flat kitchen worktop or table with easy and safe access to an electric socket. Set the glass bowl in the base. Place the lid on the bowl and push down the handle to lock it.

Plug the lead into a nearby socket and turn the timer clockwise to select the required time. At this point the power button will be on. Turn the temperature dial clockwise to the setting you want, and a light will come on. When the oven has reached the desired temperature the light will go off. It will come back on again if the temperature falls during the cooking process to indicate that the oven is heating up again. When the food is ready, which is usually indicated by a bell,

use the steel handles to take the container or racks out of the glass bowl.

The lid will be extremely hot. Do not put it directly on your kitchen worktop; instead place it on a thick cork or wooden mat.

cooking temperatures

Most halogen ovens have a lowest temperature setting of about 120°C (250°F) and a highest setting of 250°C (480°F).

You have probably noticed how similar these settings are to those of a conventional oven. However, the distinctive design of the halogen oven means that cooking times at the same temperature are greatly reduced.

which food?

You can cook almost any food in your halogen oven, and the recipes in this book include:
• Meat, poultry and fish
• Vegetables

- Pizzas and pasta
- Bread, cakes and pastry.

Don't forget that you might also have a thaw function on your halogen oven, which will enable you to cook frozen foods straight from the freezer. Even though frozen food will take longer to cook, it will still cook more quickly than in your conventional oven.

In general, vegetables will take longer to cook than meat, so you will often need to start cooking them first, particularly root vegetables. You can cook vegetables directly on the racks or in a casserole dish with a little water or oil.

take care

The oven's glass lid gets extremely hot, so always wear oven gloves to handle it and do not put it directly on your worktop.

- Always check that meat is completely cooked, because halogen ovens tend to brown meat quite quickly on the outside before cooking it through
- Use foil to avoid burning and over-browning food, removing it for the last 5 minutes of the cooking time
- Keep your halogen oven clean, washing the bowl or using the self-clean function after each use and wiping the lid with a soft, damp cloth.

chicken

pot roast chicken

1 whole chicken, about 2.5 kg (5½ lb)

50 g (2 oz) butter

4 celery sticks, halved

4 carrots

4 leeks, trimmed and washed

1 garlic clove, crushed

1 bay leaf

2 tablespoons chopped parsley

Roast Potatoes (see page 124), to serve

Put the whole chicken in a roasting tin, cover with butter and cook in the halogen oven at 200°C (400°F) for 15-20 minutes or until the skin is golden-brown.

Remove the chicken from the oven and transfer it, together with any juices, to a deep casserole dish.

Arrange the vegetables, garlic and herbs around the chicken. Add the giblets and pour water into the casserole, taking care that it does not quite cover the chicken.

Transfer the casserole dish to the lower rack in the halogen oven, still at 200°C (400°F), and bring to boiling point. Simmer gently for about 45 minutes (you may need to turn down the temperature).

Remove the chicken from the oven and discard the giblets. Serve with the vegetables and roast potatoes and offer the cooking juices as a gravy.

lemon chicken

4 chicken breasts, each
100-125 g (3½-4 oz)

2 garlic cloves, finely
chopped

½ teaspoon dried red chilli
flakes

4 lemons

To serve

couscous

Mediterranean Vegetables
(see page 128)

Put the chicken breasts in a casserole dish.

Mix together the garlic and chilli flakes and sprinkle over the chicken. Squeeze the juice from the lemons, retaining the lemon halves, and pour the juice over the chicken. Leave to marinate for at least 1 hour at room temperature.

Scatter the lemon halves over the top of the chicken. Put the casserole on the lower rack of the halogen oven and cook at 200°C (400°F) for 25-30 minutes.

Serve with couscous and Mediterranean vegetables.

simple chicken curry

4 tablespoons malt vinegar

2 teaspoons curry powder

1 teaspoon ground cumin

1 teaspoon ground coriander

¼ teaspoon ground turmeric

1 garlic clove, crushed

1 cm (½ inch) fresh root ginger, peeled and crushed

4 tablespoons demerara sugar

8 boneless, skinless chicken breasts, each 100-125 g (3½-4 oz), cubed

4 tablespoons olive oil

2 large onions, sliced

¼ teaspoon peppercorns

175 g (6 oz) ready-to-eat dried apricots, chopped

To serve

basmati rice

naan bread

In a large bowl mix together the vinegar, curry powder, cumin, coriander, turmeric, garlic, ginger and sugar.

Add the chicken pieces to this mixture and leave to marinate for 20 minutes or, for a really strong flavour, overnight.

Heat the oil in a large frying pan and cook the onions over a medium heat for about 10 minutes or until they begin to turn golden. Add the peppercorns and cook for a further 20-30 seconds.

Transfer the onions to a casserole dish and add the chicken together with any remaining marinade.

Put the casserole dish on the lower rack of the halogen oven and cook at 200°C (400°F) for about 20 minutes. Check that the chicken is cooked thoroughly and then add the apricots, cover the dish and cook for a further 5 minutes.

Serve with basmati rice and naan bread.

caribbean chicken

1 tablespoon vegetable oil

8 chicken thighs, skins on

1 large onion, chopped

3 large garlic cloves, crushed

2 cm (¾ inch) fresh root ginger, peeled and grated

1 teaspoon ground cinnamon

2 teaspoons cayenne pepper

1 tablespoon plain flour

300 ml (½ pint) hot chicken stock

750 g (1½ lb) sweet potatoes, peeled and cubed

400 ml (14 fl oz) can coconut milk

salt and pepper

boiled rice, to serve

Heat the oil in a frying pan, add the chicken thighs and brown all over. Remove the chicken with a slotted spoon and set aside. Drain all but 1 tablespoon of the oil from the pan.

Add the onion to the pan and cook over a medium heat until soft, stirring occasionally. Add the garlic, ginger, cinnamon and cayenne pepper and cook for 1 minute. Sprinkle over the flour, stir to combine and cook for a further minute.

Transfer the spice mixture to a casserole dish and stir in the stock. Add the sweet potato and chicken.

Put the casserole dish on the lower rack of the halogen oven and cook at 180°C (350°F) for 40 minutes.

Remove the dish from the halogen oven and leave to cool for a couple of minutes. Stir in the coconut milk and season to taste with salt and pepper. Serve immediately with plain boiled rice.

pesto chicken

4 boneless, skinless chicken breasts, each 100-125 g (3½-4 oz)

4 teaspoons ready-made green pesto

75 g (3 oz) Parmesan cheese, grated

12 basil leaves

3 tablespoons olive oil

500 g (1 lb) baby carrots, halved

2 peppers, deseeded and cut into chunks

1 large red onion, cut into thin wedges

salt and pepper

To serve

rocket salad

vine-ripened tomatoes

Use a sharp knife to cut a pocket in each chicken breast by slicing down one of the long sides but not cutting right through. Open up the chicken.

Spread 1 teaspoon of pesto into each pocket, adding a quarter of the Parmesan to each. Add the basil leaves, then close the pockets and secure them with cocktail sticks.

Transfer the chicken to a casserole dish and sprinkle over 2 tablespoons oil.

Add the vegetables to the casserole dish, tossing them in the oil to coat. Bring the chicken breasts to the top and season to taste with salt and pepper.

Sprinkle the remaining oil over the chicken and transfer to the lower rack of the halogen oven. Cook at 200°C (400°F) for 20-25 minutes or until the chicken is cooked and the vegetables are tender.

Serve the chicken with a peppery rocket salad and vine-ripened tomatoes.

Serves 4 Preparation time **15 minutes** Cooking time **25 minutes**

chicken stroganoff

15 g (½ oz) butter

2 teaspoons olive oil

1 small onion, finely sliced

150 g (5 oz) mushrooms, sliced

75 ml (3 fl oz) white wine

4 boneless, skinless chicken breasts, each 100–125 g (3½–4 oz), cut into strips

75 ml (3 fl oz) chicken stock

1 teaspoon wholegrain mustard

150 ml (¼ pint) soured cream

bunch of parsley or thyme, chopped

salt and pepper

To serve

new potatoes

baby carrots

Heat the butter and oil in a large frying pan, add the onion and cook for 3–4 minutes over a medium heat until soft and beginning to colour.

Add the mushrooms to the pan and cook until soft and most of the liquid has evaporated. Add the wine, bring to the boil and cook for 5 minutes to reduce by half.

Transfer the vegetables to a casserole dish and add the chicken. Place the casserole dish on the lower rack of the halogen oven and cook at 200°C (400°F) for 10 minutes or until the chicken is golden-brown.

Add the stock, mustard and soured cream and cook for a further 5 minutes or until mixture begins to boil.

Remove the top from the halogen oven and leave the chicken to rest for a couple of minutes. Season to taste with salt and pepper, sprinkle over the parsley or thyme and serve with new potatoes and baby carrots.

paprika chicken

2 red onions, cut into wedges

6 garlic cloves, unpeeled

2 teaspoons paprika

1½ tablespoons olive oil

1.75 kg (3½ lb) fresh chicken

few sprigs of rosemary

2 red peppers, cored, deseeded and cut into wide strips

2 yellow or orange peppers, cored, deseeded and cut into wide strips

300 g (10 oz) chorizo sausage, skinned if necessary and thickly sliced

4 tomatoes, halved

salt and pepper

To serve

boiled rice

tomato salad

Put the onion wedges and garlic in a large roasting tin. Stir in 1 teaspoon paprika and ½ tablespoon oil.

Place the chicken on top and brush with the remaining oil. Sprinkle over the remaining paprika and season to taste with salt and pepper.

Insert a couple of rosemary sprigs into the chicken cavity and roast the chicken on the lower rack of the halogen oven at 200°C (400°F) for 30 minutes.

Transfer the chicken to a plate and add the peppers, chorizo and tomato halves to the roasting tin. Stir to combine, then put the chicken on top of the vegetables. Cook for a further 25–30 minutes or until the chicken is cooked through and the juices run clear.

Serve with the vegetables in the roasting tin, plain boiled rice and a tomato salad.

chicken in parma ham

4 boneless, skinless chicken
breasts, each 100-125 g
(3½-4 oz)

125 g (4 oz) cream cheese
with herbs

8 slices of Parma ham

6-8 vine-ripened tomatoes

To serve

rocket leaves

new potatoes

Use a sharp knife to cut a pocket in each chicken breast by slicing down one of the long sides but not cutting right through. Fill each pocket with a quarter of the cream cheese and wrap each chicken breast with 2 slices of Parma ham.

Transfer the chicken to a casserole dish and cover them with foil. Transfer the casserole to the lower rack of the halogen oven and cook at 200°C (400°F) for 18-20 minutes or until the chicken is cooked through and the juices run clear.

After 10 minutes add the tomatoes to the oven so that they cook for 8-10 minutes.

Serve the chicken and tomatoes on a bed of rocket leaves with new potatoes.

chicken with tomatoes

4 boneless, skinless chicken
breasts, each 150-175 g
(5-6 oz)

100 g (3½ oz) cream cheese
with garlic or herbs

1 heaped teaspoon
sun-dried tomato paste

To serve

Baked Potatoes (see
page 122)

green salad

Use a sharp knife to cut each chicken breast in half horizontally but not all the way through. Open out the breasts, spread with the cream cheese and then close together. Cover the top of each piece of chicken with tomato paste.

Transfer the chicken to a casserole dish. Put the casserole on the lower rack of the halogen oven and cook at 200°C (400°F) for 18-20 minutes or until the chicken is lightly browned and cooked through. You may need to cover the top with foil to make sure the chicken does not burn.

Serve with baked potatoes and a green salad.

Makes **24 squares**   Preparation time **10 minutes**   Cooking time **10-12 minutes**

chicken & cranberry bites

375 g (12 oz) ready-rolled
flaky pastry

150 g (5 oz) cream cheese

100 g (3½ oz) cranberry
sauce

250 g (8 oz) cooked chicken
or turkey, chopped

soured cream, to serve

Cut the pastry into 24 squares and arrange them on a nonstick baking sheet. You will probably have to work in 2 batches.

Spoon a little cream cheese on to each square and add some cranberry sauce and a few chicken or turkey pieces.

Put the baking sheet on the lower rack of the halogen oven and cook at 160°C (325°F) for 10-12 minutes or until the pastry is golden-brown.

Remove the bites from the oven and leave to cool for a few minutes before serving with soured cream to dip.

pork

roast pork with crackling

875 g (1¾ lb) boneless loin of pork joint

vegetable oil, for brushing

salt

To serve

Roast Potatoes (see page 124)

carrots

Cauliflower Cheese (see page 127)

Pat the pork dry with kitchen paper and use a sharp knife to score it in a deep crisscross pattern.

Brush with oil and sprinkle generously with salt. Place the pork in a roasting tin, transfer to the lower rack of the halogen oven and cook at 200°C (400°F) for 1 hour.

Serve the pork with roast potatoes, carrots and cauliflower cheese.

herbed roast pork

4 garlic cloves, roughly chopped

leaves from 4 sprigs of rosemary

1 teaspoon ground allspice

1 tablespoon olive oil

500 g (1 lb) pork loin fillet

salt and pepper

To serve

Roast Potatoes (see page 124)

seasonal vegetables

In a bowl mix together the garlic, rosemary and allspice to make a paste. Season to taste with salt and pepper.

Rub the oil all over the pork and then rub in the paste. Cover and chill in the refrigerator for at least 30 minutes.

Transfer the seasoned pork to a baking sheet and cover with foil. Put the baking sheet on the lower rack of the halogen oven and cook at 200°C (400°F) for 35–40 minutes, removing the foil for the last 5 minutes of the cooking time.

Serve the pork with roast potatoes and a selection of seasonal vegetables of your choice.

sausage casserole

1 tablespoon oil

500 g (1 lb) new potatoes, halved

8 sausages

1 onion, chopped

1 green pepper, cored, deseeded and diced

350 g (11½ oz) ready-made tomato pasta sauce

Heat the oil in a frying pan, add the potatoes and sausages and cook over a medium heat for 5 minutes, turning the sausages from time to time so that they brown evenly. Add the onion and pepper and cook for a further 5 minutes.

Transfer the mixture to a casserole dish and stir in the pasta sauce. Put the casserole dish on the lower rack of the halogen oven, cover with foil and cook at 200°C (400°F) for 5–10 minutes. To serve, spoon on to 4 warm serving plates.

toad-in-the-hole

125 g (4 oz) plain white flour

1 teaspoon salt

3 eggs

175 ml (6 fl oz) milk

4 tablespoons vegetable oil

8 pork sausages

Onion gravy

2 teaspoons oil

225 g (8 oz) red onions, sliced

2 rounded teaspoons plain flour

450 ml (¾ pint) vegetable stock

1 teaspoon caster sugar

2 teaspoons Worcestershire sauce

Make the batter. Put the flour and salt in a large bowl, make a well in the centre and add the eggs. Mix in half the milk until the mixture is smooth, then add the remaining milk. Whisk until fully combined and the surface is covered with tiny bubbles. Set aside to rest.

Meanwhile, put the oil and sausages in a small roasting tin. Put it on the lower rack of the halogen oven and cook at 200°C (400°F) for 10-11 minutes or until the sausages are browned.

Making sure that the oil in the roasting tin is really hot, pour the batter over the sausages. Cook, still at 200°C (400°F), for 30-40 minutes or until the batter has risen and is a deep golden-brown.

Meanwhile, make the onion gravy. Heat the oil in a large frying pan and cook the onions over a medium heat for about 8 minutes.

Stir in the flour and cook for a further 1-2 minutes. Add a little of the stock at a time, stirring to make a smooth sauce, then add the remaining ingredients. Simmer for about 5 minutes.

Cut the toad-in-the-hole into 4 portions and serve with the onion gravy.

pork kebabs

40 ml (1½ fl oz) medium sherry

5 g (¼ oz) five spice powder

2 teaspoons sesame oil

1 teaspoon granulated sugar

1 garlic clove, crushed

1 teaspoon ground ginger

4 teaspoons soy sauce

350 g (11½ oz) pork fillet, cut into 2.5 cm (1 inch) cubes

1 red pepper, cored, deseeded and cut into 2.5 cm (1 inch) pieces

1 red onion, cut into 2.5 cm (1 inch) pieces

To serve

boiled rice

spring onions, finely chopped

In a small container with a lid mix together the sherry, five spice powder, sesame oil, sugar, garlic, ginger and soy sauce and shake well.

Put the pork in a plastic food bag and add the marinade. Turn to coat each piece, then transfer to the refrigerator for at least 2 hours or overnight.

Arrange pieces of pork, pepper and onion alternately on skewers. (Soak wooden skewers in water overnight so they do not burn.)

Place the skewers on the lower rack of the halogen oven and cook at 200°C (400°F) for 18–20 minutes or until the pork is cooked through. Serve with boiled rice mixed with some finely chopped spring onions.

pork burgers

450 g (14½ oz) lean pork mince

1 red dessert apple, unpeeled

1 teaspoon paprika

4 sesame-seed burger buns, halved

olive oil, for brushing

bag of mixed salad leaves

150 g (5 oz) blue cheese, cut into 4 slices

Put the mince in a large bowl. Core and finely dice the apple and add to the pork together with the paprika. Mix thoroughly with your hands and shape into 4 round burgers.

Cover the upper rack of the halogen oven with foil and arrange the burgers on the foil. Cook at 200°C (400°F) for 8-10 minutes, turning them halfway through the cooking time.

Brush the cut side of the burger buns with oil. Transfer the burgers to the lower rack and place the burger buns on the upper rack, cut side up, and cook for 1-2 minutes or until brown.

Put some salad leaves on the base of each burger bun, add a burger and top with a slice of cheese.

cider pork

2 red dessert apples, cored
and cut into wedges

4 pork loin steaks

200 ml (7 fl oz) dry cider

200 ml (7 fl oz) crème
fraîche

salt and pepper

To serve

new potatoes

seasonal vegetables

Put the apple wedges on the lower rack of the halogen oven and cook at 200°C (400°F) for 4–5 minutes. Set aside.

At the same time, season the pork steaks with salt and pepper and place them on the upper rack of the halogen oven. Cook them at 200°C (400°F) for 2–3 minutes on each side.

Pour the cider into a casserole dish, place on the lower rack of the halogen oven and cook at 250°C (480°F) for 5 minutes or until it has reduced by half.

Reduce the heat to 200°C (400°F) and stir in the crème fraîche. Add the apples and pork to the casserole dish and cook, simmering, for 5 minutes, turning halfway through the cooking time, until cooked through.

Transfer to plates. Spoon the sauce over the pork and serve with new potatoes and seasonal vegetables.

stuffed pork tenderloin

225 g (7 oz) pork tenderloin

5 g (¼ oz) toasted pine nuts, roughly chopped

5 g (¼ oz) raisins

15 g (½ oz) butter

3 thin slices of Serrano ham

olive oil, for brushing

salt and pepper

Roast Potatoes (see page 124), to serve

Use a sharp knife to make a vertical incision in the pork all the way down the middle, but do not cut all the way through. Make further cuts on each side of this incision so that you can open out the loin. Season with salt and pepper and sprinkle over the pine nuts and raisins and dot with butter.

Fold over the flaps of the pork so that the filling is fully enclosed. Wrap the ham around the pork, making sure that there are no gaps. Wrap the pork tightly in clingfilm and put it in the refrigerator for 25 minutes.

Fill a casserole dish with water, put it in the halogen oven at 250°C (480°F) and bring to the boil. Wrap the tenderloin, still in clingfilm, in foil, place in the boiling water and poach for 8-10 minutes or until the pork is just cooked. Remove the pork from the pan, remove the foil and hold under cold running water for 10 minutes.

Remove the clingfilm and dry the pork thoroughly with kitchen paper. Brush the surface of the pork with oil, and put the meat on the top rack of the halogen oven and cook at 200°C (400°F) for 5-6 minutes to brown the surface and heat through.

Cut the pork into slices and arrange on 2 plates. Serve with roast potatoes.

barbecue ribs

150 ml (¼ pint) balsamic vinegar

¼ teaspoon dried chilli flakes

1.2 kg (2½ lb) pork spare ribs

Coleslaw

4 tablespoons light mayonnaise

2 tablespoons lemon juice

1 small onion, finely sliced

½ white cabbage, finely shredded

1 carrot, roughly grated

2 celery sticks, finely sliced diagonally

salt and pepper

Make the glaze. Put the balsamic vinegar and chilli flakes into a small saucepan over a high heat. Bring to the boil, reduce the heat and simmer for about 5 minutes or until reduced by half and slightly thickened.

Make the coleslaw. Put the mayonnaise in a bowl, stir in the lemon juice and season well with salt and pepper. Add the onion, cabbage, carrot and celery and mix together.

Brush the glaze over the ribs and arrange them on the upper rack in the halogen oven. Cook at 200°C (400°F) for 10 minutes. Arrange the cooked ribs on 4 plates and serve with the coleslaw.

A halogen oven with baking racks and handle

Removing a cooking rack from an oven using the handles

Drying a washed bowl with a clean cloth

Paprika Chicken (see page 18)

roasted pork with orange

4 thick slices of white bread, crusts removed

juice and finely grated rind of 1 orange

4 sprigs of thyme

2 pork tenderloin fillets, each about 450 g (14½ oz)

2 teaspoons cornflour

300 ml (½ pint) vegetable or chicken stock

Roast Potatoes (see page 124), to serve

Whizz the bread in a food processor to make breadcrumbs. Transfer to a bowl and mix with the orange rind and thyme.

Lay each piece of pork on a board and use a sharp knife to make a deep slit along the length to create a pocket. Fill the pockets with the breadcrumb mixture and secure with cocktail sticks.

Place the pork in a roasting tin and transfer to the lower rack of the halogen oven. Cook at 200°C (400°F) for 15-20 minutes or until cooked through. Remove the pork from the oven, transfer to a plate and cover with foil.

In a small bowl mix the orange juice with the cornflour to make a smooth paste. Put the paste in the roasting tin with the pork juices and heat on the hob over a high heat. Add the stock and bring to the boil, stirring, then simmer for 3-4 minutes until thickened.

Remove the cocktail sticks from the pork and slice the meat on to 4 plates. Drizzle over the sauce and serve with roast potatoes.

lamb

rack of lamb

6 tablespoons clear honey

3 tablespoons light soy sauce

2 tablespoons English mustard

2 tablespoons chopped mint

2 x 6-bone lean racks of lamb

salt and pepper

To serve

Roast Potatoes (see page 124)

green beans

carrots

In a bowl mix together the honey, soy sauce, mustard and mint.

Put the racks of lamb, fat side up, on a chopping board. Season to taste on both sides with salt and pepper and brush on both sides with the honey mixture. Transfer to a foil-lined baking sheet.

Put the racks of lamb on the lower rack of the halogen oven and cook at 200°C (400°F) for 30-35 minutes. Remember to cover the racks of lamb with foil if they look as if they are burning.

Divide the lamb and transfer to 4 plates. Serve with roast potatoes, green beans and carrots.

sticky chops

6 lamb chops, each 50-65 g
(2-2½ oz)

green salad, to serve

Sticky marinade

2 tablespoons white wine
vinegar

½ teaspoon ground nutmeg

2 garlic cloves, crushed

1 tablespoon light brown
sugar

4 tablespoons plum jam

5 tablespoons tomato
ketchup

1 tablespoon soy sauce
(optional)

1 tablespoon sweet chilli
sauce (optional)

salt and pepper

In a large, non-metallic bowl mix together all the ingredients for the marinade, making sure they are thoroughly combined.

Add the chops to the bowl and turn them to coat completely in the marinade. Cover and transfer to the refrigerator for at least 2 hours or overnight.

Put the chops on the upper rack in the halogen oven and cook at 200°C (400°F) for 10-15 minutes, turning occasionally. Serve with a green salad.

lamb shanks

olive oil, for braising

2 lamb shanks

1 leek, roughly chopped

2 celery sticks, roughly chopped

2 carrots, roughly chopped

2 onions, roughly chopped

1 whole head of garlic, cloves separated but unpeeled

375 ml (12 fl oz) red wine

600 ml (1 pint) chicken stock

Pour olive oil into a casserole dish to a depth of 1 cm (½ inch) and heat on the hob over a high heat until the oil is sizzling. Add the lamb shanks and cook, turning occasionally, until brown.

Remove the lamb shanks from the casserole with a slotted spoon and add the leek, celery, carrots, onions and garlic. Cook for 10-12 minutes or until they begin to soften.

Return the lamb to the casserole, arranging the shanks on top of the vegetables. Add the red wine and chicken stock and bring to the boil.

Transfer the casserole dish to the lower rack of the halogen oven, cover with foil and cook at 180°C (350°F) for 1 hour. Check that the meat is falling off the bone; if not, cook for a further 20 minutes.

Serve the lamb with the vegetables and with the cooking juices poured over the top.

curried lamb kebabs

450 g (14½ oz) lean lamb mince

2 teaspoons ground cumin

2 teaspoons ground turmeric

1 tablespoon sunflower oil

2 garlic cloves, crushed

½ teaspoon caster sugar

boiled rice, to serve

Dip

200 ml (7 fl oz) Greek yogurt

4 tablespoons mint jelly

Put the mince in a large bowl. Add the cumin, turmeric, oil, garlic and sugar and mix well. Cover and leave in the refrigerator for 2 hours or overnight.

Use the spicy mince mixture to form 10-12 sausages around the skewers. Remember to soak wooden skewers in water before use so that they do not burn during cooking.

Arrange the kebabs on the upper rack of the halogen oven and cook at 200°C (400°F) for 12-15 minutes.

Meanwhile, mix together the yogurt and mint jelly in a bowl. Serve the skewers with the dip and accompanied by boiled rice.

lamb hotpot

450 g (14½ oz) lean lamb mince

125 g (4 oz) mushrooms, sliced

450 ml (¾ pint) hot lamb stock

2 tablespoons gravy granules

1 tablespoon thyme leaves

2 leeks, finely sliced

50 g (2 oz) Lancashire cheese, grated

750 g (1½ lb) potatoes, sliced

melted butter

salt and pepper

In a large, nonstick frying pan over a medium heat dry-fry the mince with the mushrooms for 4-5 minutes until evenly browned. Add the stock, gravy granules and thyme and cook for further 2-3 minutes until thickened. Season to taste with salt and pepper and transfer to a casserole dish.

Cover the mince with the leeks and cheese and then layer the potatoes over the top. Brush the potatoes with melted butter and cover with foil.

Place the casserole dish on the lower rack of the halogen oven and cook at 180°C (350°F) for 25 minutes, removing the foil for the last 5-10 minutes to allow the potatoes to brown.

Serves 2   Preparation time **10 minutes**   Cooking time **10-15 minutes**

lamb mixed grill

4 lamb loin chops

4 beef sausages

2 tomatoes, halved

2 large mushrooms

25-30 g (1-1¼ oz) butter

salt and pepper

Chunky Chips (see page 123), to serve

Arrange the chops, sausages, tomatoes and mushrooms on a baking sheet. Put some of the butter on each mushroom. Season to taste with salt and pepper.

Put the baking sheet on the lower rack of the halogen oven and cook at 200°C (400°F) for 10-15 minutes, turning the chops and sausages about halfway through the cooking time.

Transfer the mixed grill to 2 warm plates and serve with homemade chips.

Serves **4**   Preparation time **10 minutes**   Cooking time **4–5 minutes**

spicy lamb meatballs

450 g (14½ oz) lamb mince

1 small onion, finely chopped

¼ teaspoon ground allspice

¼ teaspoon juniper berries, crushed

1 sprig of thyme, leaves roughly chopped

2 tablespoons currants

3 tablespoons olive oil

tagliatelle, to serve

Put the lamb in a large bowl and add the onion, allspice, juniper berries, thyme and currants. Mix the ingredients together thoroughly and then form the mixture into 15–20 small balls, each about the size of a golf ball.

Brush the bottom of a casserole dish with oil and arrange the meatballs in the dish. Place on the lower rack of the halogen oven and cook at 200°C (400°F) for 4–5 minutes.

Serve with pasta, such as tagliatelle, cooked according to the instructions on the packet.

lamb with spicy sausage

450 g (14½ oz) lean lamb, cut into 2.5 cm (1 inch) cubes

2 tablespoons plain flour seasoned with salt and pepper

2 tablespoons olive oil

100 g (3½ oz) chorizo or spicy paprika sausage, skinned and cut into large pieces

1 red onion, finely chopped

2 garlic cloves, crushed

300 ml (½ pint) hot lamb stock

150 ml (¼ pint) red wine

410 g (13¼ oz) can black-eye peas or butter beans, rinsed and drained

Sweet Potato Wedges (see page 123), to serve

Coat the lamb in the seasoned flour.

Heat the oil in a large, nonstick frying pan and cook the lamb and chorizo over a medium heat for 3-4 minutes or until brown. Transfer to a large, ovenproof casserole dish; the casserole should hold about 3 litres (5½ pints) but check first that it will fit inside your halogen oven.

In the same frying pan cook the onions and garlic until soft. Transfer to the casserole together with the stock and wine.

Cook on the lower rack of the halogen oven at 200°C (400°F) for 22-25 minutes, stirring occasionally. About 10 minutes before the end of the cooking time add the beans and reduce the heat to 160°C (325°F).

Serve the lamb with sweet potato wedges.

lamb stew

1 kg (2 lb) lean boneless lamb shoulder, cubed

2 bay leaves

4 sprigs of thyme

1 onion, quartered

1 leek, roughly chopped

3 garlic cloves, crushed

1.2 litres (2 pints) cold water

200 g (7 oz) baby carrots

200 g (7 oz) baby turnips

200 g (7 oz) baby onions or shallots

200 g (7 oz) small leeks

200 ml (7 fl oz) white wine (dry or medium)

200 ml (7 fl oz) hot lamb stock

200 g (7 oz) green beans, trimmed

200 g (7 oz) peas

salt and pepper

mashed potato, to serve

Place the lamb in a roasting tin with the bay leaves, thyme, onion, leek, garlic and water. Season to taste with salt and pepper and cover with foil.

Put the roasting tin on the lower rack of the halogen oven and cook at 200°C (400°F) for 15 minutes.

Transfer the lamb to a large casserole dish and strain the vegetable juices over the meat, discarding the vegetables and herbs.

Add the carrots, turnips, onions or shallots, leeks, white wine and stock to the lamb. Place the casserole on the lower rack of the halogen oven and cook at 250°C (480°F) for 10 minutes.

Add the green beans to the casserole and cook for a further 2 minutes. Add the peas and cook for a further 2 minutes or until the vegetables are cooked. Serve with mashed potato.

lamb ragout

1 tablespoon olive oil

675 g (1 lb 6 oz) boneless lamb shoulder, leg or neck fillet, cut into 2.5 cm (1 inch) cubes

grated rind of 1 lemon

2 garlic cloves, crushed

6 spring onions, finely chopped

150 ml (¼ pint) cider or white wine

600 ml (1 pint) hot lamb or vegetable stock

2 bay leaves

100 g (3½ oz) sweet corn kernels

75 g (3 oz) cauliflower florets

2 courgettes, roughly chopped

75 g (3 oz) sugar snap peas

small handful of chopped mint leaves

salt and pepper

new potatoes, to serve

Heat the oil in a large ovenproof casserole dish, add the lamb, lemon rind and garlic and cook, stirring occasionally, over a medium heat for 4-5 minutes until brown. Transfer to a plate.

Add the spring onions to the same casserole dish and cook for 1-2 minutes until soft. Return the lamb to the casserole and add the cider or wine, hot stock and bay leaves.

Transfer the casserole to the lower rack of the halogen oven and cook at 200°C (400°F) for 20 minutes.

Add the sweet corn, cauliflower and courgettes and cook for a further 5-10 minutes.

Season to taste with salt and pepper, stir through the sugar snap peas and mint and serve immediately with new potatoes.

beef

Serves **6** Preparation time **5 minutes** Cooking time **45–50 minutes**

traditional roast beef

1.25 kg (2½ lb) lean topside joint

3 red onions, cut into wedges

10 garlic cloves, unpeeled

To serve

Roast Potatoes (see page 124)

seasonal vegetables

Put the beef on a small baking sheet on the upper rack in the halogen oven and cook at 200°C (400°F) for 45–50 minutes.

After 20 minutes add the red onions and garlic to the base of the oven and place the beef on top of the vegetables.

Remove the beef from the oven and leave it to rest for 5–10 minutes then serve with the onions and garlic, roast potatoes and seasonal vegetables.

Pork Kebabs (see page 28)

Cooking racks of lamb in a halogen oven

Rack of Lamb (see page 40)

Lamb Ragout (see page 49)

spicy steaks

675 g (1 lb 6 oz) lean thin
steaks

Spicy marinade

4 garlic cloves, finely
chopped

1 red chilli, deseeded and
finely chopped

juice of 1 orange

juice of 1 lemon

2 tablespoons chopped flat
leaf parsley

3 tablespoons olive oil

salt and pepper

To serve

green salad

Chunky Chips (see
page 123)

Make the marinade. Mix together all the ingredients in a large, non-metallic dish. Add the steaks to the mixture, turning them to coat both sides. Cover and refrigerate for at least 1 hour.

Place the steaks directly on the upper rack of the halogen oven and cook at 200°C (400°F) for 3–4 minutes (medium rare), 5–6 minutes (medium) and 10 minutes or more for well done.

Serve the steaks with homemade chips and a fresh green salad.

beef stew with dumplings

1 tablespoon vegetable oil

450 g (14½ oz) lean braising steak, cubed

2 celery sticks, chopped

6 baby carrots, left whole

½ small swede, chopped

2 parsnips, chopped

600 ml (1 pint) hot beef stock

1 tablespoon Worcestershire sauce

2 tablespoons gravy granules

Dumplings

100 g (3½ oz) self-raising flour

50 g (2 oz) suet

1 tablespoon wholegrain mustard

75 ml (3 fl oz) water

To serve

carrots

broccoli

Heat the oil in a frying pan and cook the braising steak for 4–5 minutes until browned on all sides.

Transfer the meat to a casserole dish and add the celery, carrots, swede and parsnips. Pour over the stock and stir in the Worcestershire sauce.

Cover the casserole with foil, place on the lower rack of the halogen oven and cook at 160°C (320°F) for 40 minutes or until the beef is tender.

Meanwhile, make the dumplings. Mix together the flour, suet, mustard and water in a bowl to form a smooth dough. Divide it into 8 equal pieces and form them into balls.

After the beef has been cooking for 20 minutes remove the casserole from the oven. Remove the foil and stir in the gravy granules and arrange the dumplings on top.

Return the casserole dish, uncovered, to the halogen oven and cook at 200°C (400°F) for the remaining 20 minutes. Serve with buttered carrots and broccoli.

red pepper burgers

450 g (14½ oz) lean beef mince

1 small onion, finely grated

1 garlic clove, crushed

1 small red pepper, deseeded and finely diced

½ teaspoon dried mixed herbs

2 tablespoons sweet chilli sauce

25-50 g (1-2 oz) fresh breadcrumbs

1 egg, beaten

1 tablespoon sunflower or vegetable oil

salt and pepper

To serve

burger buns

salad leaves

tomato slices

red onion slices

mayonnaise

Put the beef in a large bowl and combine it with the onion, garlic, red pepper, herbs, sweet chilli sauce and breadcrumbs. Season to taste with salt and pepper and mix in the egg. Mix together thoroughly, cover and refrigerate for 30 minutes.

Shape the mixture into 4-6 even-sized burgers. Brush each burger with oil and cook on the upper rack of the halogen oven at 200°C (400°F) for 10-11 minutes.

Serve the burgers in the split buns with salad leaves, slices of tomato and red onion and mayonnaise.

beef-stuffed peppers

3 large red peppers

1 tablespoon olive oil

375 g (12 oz) lean beef mince

200 ml (7 fl oz) tomato passata

½ small onion, finely chopped

2 garlic cloves, finely chopped

1 celery stick, finely chopped

1 tablespoon chopped oregano

50 g (2 oz) reduced-fat cheese, grated

salt and pepper

sprigs of thyme, to garnish

Cut the peppers in half at the longest point and remove the cores and seeds. Place them on a baking sheet and brush with oil. Put the baking sheet on the lower rack of the halogen oven and roast at 200°C (400°F) for 10 minutes.

Meanwhile, put the mince in a large frying pan and dry-fry over a medium heat until the mince is brown. Drain away any juices and transfer the meat to a bowl.

Add the passata, onion, garlic, celery and oregano and season to taste with salt and pepper. Mix together thoroughly.

Remove the peppers from the halogen oven and divide the filling among them. Place the peppers on the lower rack, cover with foil and cook at 160°C (325°F) for a further 5–10 minutes.

Remove the foil from the peppers, sprinkle over the cheese and return the peppers to the oven for a further 2 minutes or until the cheese has melted. Serve immediately, garnished with thyme sprigs.

chilli roast beef

1.5–2 kg (3–4 lb) lean beef joint

salt and pepper

Marinade

1 teaspoon dried chilli flakes

2 garlic cloves, crushed

1 tablespoon fresh root ginger, finely chopped

3 tablespoons chopped chives

2 tablespoons sherry vinegar

To serve

Dauphinoise Potatoes (see page 122)

seasonal vegetables

Put the beef on a chopping board and lightly score the surface with a sharp knife.

Transfer the meat to a non-metallic dish and season to taste with salt and pepper.

Make the marinade. Mix together all the ingredients and rub the mixture all over the joint. Cover and marinate in the refrigerator for 2 hours or overnight.

Take the joint out of the refrigerator and discard any excess marinade. Put the beef on the lower rack of the halogen oven and cook at 200°C (400°F) for 45–50 minutes, covering the meat with foil if it looks as if it is drying out.

Remove the beef from the oven and leave it to rest for about 10 minutes then slice and serve with dauphinoise potatoes and seasonal vegetables.

steak & kidney pies

1 tablespoon sunflower oil

450 g (14½ oz) lean braising or stewing steak, cubed

1 onion, sliced

100 g (3½ oz) chestnut mushrooms, quartered

225 g (7½ oz) ox kidney, cored, trimmed and cut into small chunks

1 tablespoon plain flour

450 ml (¾ pint) hot beef stock

200 ml (7 fl oz) ale

500 g (1 lb) short crust pastry (thawed if frozen)

1 egg, beaten

salt and pepper

To serve

peas

Chunky Chips (see page 123)

Heat the oil in a large frying pan and cook the beef over a medium heat for 3–4 minutes until brown on all sides.

Add the onion and mushrooms to the pan and cook for a further 4–5 minutes until coloured. Add the kidneys and cook for 1–2 minutes. Sprinkle over the flour.

Transfer the meat and vegetables to a casserole dish and add the stock and ale. Season to taste with salt and pepper. Put the casserole on the lower rack of the halogen oven, cover with foil and cook at 200°C (400°F) for 45–50 minutes or until the meat is tender. Spoon the cooked mixture into 2 individual pie dishes.

Roll out the pastry and cut out 2 lids slightly larger than each dish. Place the pastry lid on top of the meat filling, dampening the edges of each dish. Trim away the excess pastry and press the edges to seal. Brush the tops with egg and cook the pies at 230°C (450°F) for 20–25 minutes or until the pastry is golden, covering the pastry for the first 10–15 minutes so that it does not burn.

Divide the pies in half and serve with garden peas and homemade chips.

chilli

1 tablespoon oil

2 onions, finely chopped

2 large garlic cloves, crushed

750 g (1½ lb) lean beef mince

150 ml (¼ pint) red wine

2 x 400 g (13 oz) cans chopped tomatoes

2-3 tablespoons tomato purée

2 teaspoons dried chilli flakes, plus extra to serve

1-2 tablespoons sweet chilli sauce

2 teaspoons ground cumin

2 teaspoons ground coriander

1 teaspoon ground ginger

1-2 bay leaves

2 tablespoons good quality cocoa powder

1 beef stock cube

2 x 400 g (13 oz) cans red kidney beans, rinsed and drained

salt and pepper

boiled rice, to serve

Heat the oil in a large, nonstick frying pan and cook the onions and garlic over a medium heat for 1-2 minutes.

Add the mince and cook for a few minutes until brown. Add the wine and cook for a further 2-3 minutes.

Transfer the mince mixture to a casserole dish and stir in the tomatoes, tomato purée, chilli flakes, sweet chilli sauce, spices, bay leaves and cocoa powder. Crumble over the stock cube and season to taste with salt and pepper. Stir to mix.

Put the casserole dish in the halogen oven and cook at 200°C (400°F) for 30 minutes. Add the red kidney beans and cook for a further 10 minutes.

Serve with plain boiled rice and a sprinkling of dried chilli flakes.

steak with tangy sauce

2 sirloin, rump, rib-eye or fillet steaks

2 teaspoons olive oil

green salad, to serve

Tangy sauce

2 tablespoons olive oil

2 garlic cloves, finely chopped

100 ml (3½ fl oz) sweet sherry

100 ml (3½ fl oz) red wine

100 ml (3½ fl oz) hot beef stock or water

1 tablespoon tomato purée

pinch of dried chilli flakes (optional)

2 tablespoons chopped chives

salt and pepper

Make the sauce. Heat the oil in a frying pan, add the garlic and cook over a medium heat until soft. Add the sherry and wine, bring to the boil, reduce the heat and cook, stirring, for 10–15 minutes until the sauce has thickened.

Stir in the stock or water, tomato purée and chilli flakes, if using. Season to taste with salt and pepper. Add the chives, increase the heat and boil the sauce for a couple of minutes to thicken.

Meanwhile, put the steaks on the upper rack of the halogen oven and brush with a little oil. Cook at 200°C (400°F) for 15 minutes for a well-done steak, reducing the time if you prefer your meat less well done.

Serve the steaks with a little of the sauce poured over and a crisp green salad.

thai beef curry

300 ml (½ pint) coconut milk

300 ml (½ pint) water

2 tablespoons Thai red curry paste

1 stalk of lemon grass, sliced thinly

4 dried or fresh kaffir lime leaves

1 tablespoon lime juice

1 tablespoon Thai fish sauce (nam pla)

450 g (14½ oz) lean rump steak, trimmed of any fat and thinly sliced

225 g (7½ oz) shallots, sliced

150 g (5 oz) carrots, thinly sliced

175 g (6 oz) sugar snap peas

175 g (6 oz) cherry tomatoes, halved

3 tablespoons chopped coriander leaves

Pilau Rice (see page 125), to serve

Pour the coconut milk and water into a large saucepan. Add the curry paste, lemon grass, kaffir lime leaves, lime juice and fish sauce, bring to the boil and boil quickly for 2 minutes.

Transfer the coconut milk mixture to a casserole dish and add the meat and shallots. Place on the upper rack of the halogen oven and cook at 200°C (400°F) for 10 minutes.

Add the carrots and sugar snap peas to the curry and cook for a further 8-10 minutes. Stir in the tomatoes and coriander and cook for a further 2 minutes.

Serve the curry with pilau rice.

fish &
seafood

salmon fishcakes

750 g (1½ lb) potatoes, cut into large chunks

25-30 g (1-1¼ oz) butter

210 g (7½ oz) can red salmon, drained

2 tablespoons chopped parsley

1 egg, beaten

1 tablespoon flour

salt and pepper

To serve

lettuce leaves

lemon wedges

Cook the potatoes in a large saucepan of boiling water for 10-12 minutes or until they are tender. Drain and return to the pan.

Mash the potatoes with the butter and stir in the salmon and parsley. Season to taste with salt and pepper and mix with sufficient egg for the mixture to bind together. Divide the mixture into 12 equal portions and shape them into patties.

Cover each fishcake in a light coating of flour and place them on the lower rack of the halogen oven. Cook at 250°C (480°F) for 8-10 minutes or until golden-brown, covering them with foil for the first 5 minutes so that they don't burn.

Serve the fishcakes on a bed of crisp lettuce with lemon wedges to squeeze over.

mushroom-stuffed plaice

4 whole plaice

1 tablespoon oil

1 onion, finely chopped

1 garlic clove, crushed

75 g (3 oz) brown breadcrumbs

100 g (3½ oz) mushrooms, finely chopped

1 tomato, peeled and chopped

1 teaspoon chopped marjoram

2 teaspoons chopped parsley

dash of Worcestershire sauce

sprigs of watercress, to garnish

To serve

grilled tomatoes

grilled mushrooms

Put the fish, skin side down, on a board. Use a sharp knife to cut 2 pockets into the sides of each fish. Do this by making a cut down the backbone. On one half cut two-thirds of the way around to form a pocket; repeat on the other half.

Make the mushroom filling. Heat the oil in a large frying pan. Add the onion, garlic and breadcrumbs and fry over a medium heat until the breadcrumbs are crisp. Stir in the mushrooms, tomato, herbs and Worcestershire sauce and fry for 2 further minutes.

Stuff the fish with the filling, arrange them in a buttered ovenproof dish and cover with foil. Cook on the upper rack of the halogen oven at 250°C (480°F) for 8-10 minutes.

Transfer the fish to serving plates and garnish with the watercress. Serve immediately with grilled tomatoes and mushrooms.

crusty salmon

4 salmon fillets, each about 125 g (4 oz)

2 tablespoons olive oil

100 g (3½ oz) oatmeal

rind of 1 large lemon

3 tablespoons chopped herbs, such as parsley or dill

salt and pepper

To serve

new potatoes

green salad

Brush the salmon all over with oil.

Combine the oatmeal, lemon rind and herbs in a bowl and season to taste with salt and pepper.

Tip the oatmeal mixture on to a plate. Dip the rounded surface of each salmon fillet into the oatmeal mixture and transfer to a small baking sheet. Cook on the upper rack of the halogen oven at 250°C (480°F) for 8-10 minutes.

Serve the salmon immediately with new potatoes and a crisp green salad.

honey & sesame salmon

1 tablespoon clear honey

2 tablespoons soy sauce

2 salmon fillets, each about
150 g (5 oz)

2 tablespoons chopped
spring onions

2 tablespoons sesame seeds

To serve

new potatoes

rocket leaves

In a bowl mix together the honey and soy sauce. Drizzle the honey mixture over the salmon fillet.

Sprinkle the salmon with chopped spring onions and roll them in sesame seeds. Transfer them, skin side down, to a foil-lined baking sheet.

Cook the salmon on the upper rack of the halogen oven at 250°C (480°F) for 8–10 minutes.

Serve immediately with new potatoes and a peppery rocket salad.

tuna with salsa

4 tuna steaks, each
125-150 g (4-5 oz)

1 tablespoon olive oil

salt and pepper

Salsa

2 ripe nectarines or peaches

1 small red onion, finely
diced

1 green chilli, deseeded and
finely chopped

2 tablespoons chopped
mint

2 tablespoons chopped basil

rind and juice of 1 lime

1 teaspoon olive oil

To serve

green salad

lime wedges

Make the salsa. Remove the skins and stones from the peaches or nectarines. Chop the flesh, put the pieces in a bowl and mix in the onion, chilli, herbs, lime rind and juice and oil. Set aside.

Brush the tuna with oil and season to taste with salt and pepper.

Place 2 of the tuna steaks on the upper rack of the halogen oven and cook at 250°C (480°F) for 2 minutes each side. Repeat with the remaining tuna.

Serve with green salad, the salsa and lime wedges to squeeze over the fish.

Serves **4** Preparation time **15 minutes** Cooking time **25-30 minutes**

tuna pasta bake

2 x 185 g (6¼ oz) cans tuna in brine

1 tablespoon olive oil, plus extra for greasing

4 spring onions or 1 small onion, finely chopped

300 g (10 oz) small pasta shapes, such as penne

600 ml (1 pint) milk

25 g (1 oz) plain flour

25 g (1 oz) butter

125 g (4 oz) mature Cheddar cheese, grated

1 teaspoon mustard

½ teaspoon lemon juice

Garlic bread

2 small, part-baked baguettes

1 garlic clove, halved

25 g (1 oz) butter

Drain the tuna and flake the flesh into a bowl.

Heat the oil in a frying pan and cook the spring onions or onion over a medium heat for a couple of minutes to soften.

Meanwhile, cook the pasta in a large saucepan of boiling water according to the instructions on the packet. Drain and set aside.

Put the milk, flour and butter in a small saucepan and whisk constantly over a medium heat until the sauce begins to boil and thicken. Turn down the heat to its lowest and let the sauce cook very gently for 2 minutes. Add about 75 g (3 oz) grated cheese and the mustard and lemon juice.

Mix the pasta with the spring onions or onion, tuna and cheese sauce and pour into a lightly oiled 1.2-1.5 litre (2-2½ pint) casserole dish.

Sprinkle over the remaining cheese and bake on the lower rack of the halogen oven at 200°C (400°F) for about 20 minutes or until the top is golden.

Meanwhile, make garlic bread by cutting each baguette in half lengthways. Rub the cut surfaces with garlic and spread with butter. Bake on the upper rack of the halogen oven at 200° (400°F) for 6-8 minutes.

Spoon the pasta bake on to warm plates and serve with chunks of garlic bread.

baked halibut

500 g (1 lb) small waxy new potatoes, thinly sliced

2 tablespoons olive oil, plus extra for drizzling

500 g (1 lb) frozen Ratatouille (see page 129)

1 red chilli, deseeded and finely chopped or a generous pinch of chilli flakes

4 halibut steaks, each about 200 g (7 oz)

1 lemon, sliced

salt and pepper

bread and butter, to serve

Put the potatoes in a large bowl. Pour over the oil and season to taste with salt and pepper. Turn to coat the slices evenly.

Arrange the potato slices in layers on a large baking sheet, place on the lower rack of the halogen oven and cook at 250°C (480°F) for 20-25 minutes or until turning golden.

Spoon the frozen ratatouille over the potatoes and sprinkle with the chilli. Put the halibut on top of the ratatouille and arrange the lemon slices over the fish.

Season to taste with salt and pepper and cook on the upper rack of the halogen oven at 250°C (480°F) for 8-10 minutes or until the fish is cooked through. Serve with chunky bread and butter.

tandoori prawns

4 tablespoons natural yogurt

2 tablespoons tandoori curry paste

450 g (14½ oz) large uncooked peeled prawns

125 g (4 oz) basmati rice

Raita

½ cucumber

100 g (3½ oz) natural yogurt

a handful of chopped mint leaves

salt and pepper

To garnish

sprigs of mint

lime wedges (optional)

In a bowl mix together the yogurt and curry paste. Add the prawns and turn to coat thoroughly.

Arrange the prawns in a single layer on a foil-covered baking sheet and pour over any remaining marinade. Place the prawns on the upper rack of the halogen oven and cook at 250°C (480°F) for 4-5 minutes.

Meanwhile, cook the rice according to the instructions on the packet.

Make the raita. Use a vegetable peeler to cut long, thin strips from the cucumber and pat them dry on kitchen paper. Transfer the cucumber to a bowl and add the yogurt and mint. Season to taste with salt and pepper and mix together.

Serve the prawns, garnished with mint sprigs and lime wedges, if liked, and accompanied with the rice and raita.

Serves 4   Preparation time **15 minutes**   Cooking time **13–20 minutes**

prawn & salmon pie

625 g (1¼ lb) salmon fillet, skinned and cut into 2.5 cm (1 inch pieces)

250 g (8 oz) uncooked peeled prawns

250 ml (8 fl oz) ready-made parsley sauce

2–3 large handfuls of baby spinach leaves, washed

175 g (6 oz) ready-to-roll puff pastry

1 egg, beaten

salt and pepper

Put the salmon and prawns in a casserole dish. Pour the sauce into the casserole and mix gently to combine. Season to taste with salt and pepper.

Transfer the casserole dish to the upper rack of the halogen oven and cook at 250°C (480°F) until just bubbling. Reduce the heat to 200°C (400°F) and cook for a further 8–10 minutes or until the fish is cooked through.

Add the spinach and cook for a couple of minutes until the leaves have begun to wilt.

Meanwhile, roll out the pastry and cut it into 4 equal pieces. Place these on a small nonstick baking sheet and use a knife to score each with a crisscross pattern. Brush with a little egg. Move the fish to the lower rack and cook the pastry on the upper rack for 5–10 minutes or until well risen and golden, covering it with foil for the first 5 minutes so that it doesn't burn.

Spoon the fish mixture on to 4 plates and serve each one topped with a piece of pastry.

Serves 4   Preparation time **10 minutes**   Cooking time **22 minutes**

haddock & broccoli pie

350 g (11½ oz) broccoli, divided into florets

450 g (14½ oz) smoked haddock, cut into chunks

1 packet of parsley sauce

4 sheets of filo pastry (thawed if frozen)

50 g (2 oz) butter, melted

To serve

Roast Potatoes (see page 124)

peas

Bring a large saucepan of lightly salted water to the boil. Add the broccoli to the water to blanch it, remove it, drain and refresh under cold water. Drain again.

Put the broccoli and haddock in the base of a casserole dish. Make up the sauce according to the instructions on the packet and spoon over enough to cover the broccoli and haddock.

Brush a sheet of filo pastry with melted butter. Tear it into 4 strips and drape them over the fish and broccoli. Repeat with the other 3 sheets of pastry until the fish and broccoli are completely covered. (You may not need to use all the pastry.)

Cover the pie with foil and cook in the halogen oven and cook at 250°C (480°F) for about 15 minutes. Remove the foil and cook for a further 5 minutes or until the pastry is golden and the filling begins to bubble.

Transfer the pie to 4 serving plates and serve with roast potatoes and peas.

pasta & pizzas

Serves 2   Preparation time **10 minutes**   Cooking time **about 10 minutes**

lamb pasta

225 g (7½ oz) lamb leg steaks

50 g (2 oz) asparagus, sliced

1 courgette, sliced

100 g (3½ oz) peas

150 g (5 oz) pasta ribbons

3 teaspoons olive oil

1 tablespoon mint sauce

2 tablespoons clear honey

sprigs of mint, to garnish

Cut the lamb into thin strips and put the meat in a casserole dish. Cook on the lower rack of the halogen oven at 200°C (400°F) for 3-4 minutes or until the meat has browned.

Add the asparagus, courgette and peas to the casserole dish and cook for a further 3-4 minutes.

Meanwhile, cook the pasta in boiling water according to the instructions on the packet. Drain and mix together the oil, mint sauce and honey and add to the casserole dish.

Combine the lamb, pasta and vegetables and heat for a further couple of minutes, still on the lower rack.

Serve the pasta in warm bowls, garnished with mint sprigs.

chilli pasta bake

450 g (14½ oz) lean beef mince

1 onion, finely chopped

2 celery sticks, finely chopped

1 small red chilli, deseeded and finely chopped

200 g (7 oz) dried pasta shapes

150 g (5 oz) chestnut mushrooms, sliced

2 large sprigs of thyme, roughly chopped

2 tablespoons sweet sherry

50 g (2 oz) mozzarella cheese, grated

25 g (1 oz) Parmesan cheese, grated

500 ml (17 fl oz) hot beef gravy

2 tablespoons chopped flat leaf parsley, to garnish

salt and pepper

To serve

green salad

Garlic Bread (see page 73)

Put the mince, onion, celery and chilli in a large, nonstick frying pan and dry-fry over a medium heat until brown.

Meanwhile, cook the pasta according to the instructions on the packet. Drain and set aside.

Add the mushrooms, thyme and sherry to the mince and season to taste with salt and pepper.

Mix together the mozzarella and Parmesan.

Transfer the mince mixture to a casserole dish and stir in the gravy. Put the casserole on the lower rack of the halogen oven and cook at 200°C (400°F) for 10 minutes.

Combine the pasta with the mince, add half the cheese mixture and stir to mix. Sprinkle over the remaining cheese and cook on the lower rack at 180°C (350°F) for a further 10–15 minutes.

Serve immediately with a crisp green salad and chunks of warm garlic bread.

Serves **4**   Preparation time **5 minutes**   Cooking time **10–12 minutes**

pork pasta with lemon

500 g (1 lb) small pasta shapes

6 pork sausages

grated rind and juice of 1 lemon

pinch of dried chilli flakes

200 ml (7 fl oz) half-fat crème fraîche

50 g (2 oz) Parmesan cheese, grated, to serve

Cook the pasta according to the instructions on the packet. Drain thoroughly.

Meanwhile, split the skins of the sausages and transfer the meat to a casserole dish, discarding the skins and breaking up the meat with a fork.

Cook the sausagemeat on the lower rack of the halogen oven at 250°C (480°F) for 8-10 minutes or until golden and crispy.

Add the lemon rind, lemon juice (to taste), chilli flakes and the crème fraîche, stir and cook for a further couple of minutes until the sauce is bubbling.

Toss the pasta and meat together to combine and serve with grated Parmesan.

sausage pasta bake

8 pork and herb sausages, cut into chunks

350 g (11½ oz) ready-made tomato and roasted vegetables pasta sauce

350 g (11½ oz) dried penne pasta

handful of torn basil leaves

150 g (5 oz) mozzarella cheese, drained and diced

salt and pepper

50 g (2 oz) Parmesan cheese, grated, to serve

Cook the sausage chunks on the upper rack of the halogen oven at 200°C (400°F) for 4-5 minutes or until brown.

Transfer the sausage to a casserole dish and add the pasta sauce. Cook on the lower rack of the halogen oven at 200°C (400°F) for 10 minutes. Season to taste with salt and pepper.

Meanwhile, cook the pasta according to the instructions on the packet. Drain thoroughly and add to the casserole dish.

Scatter the mozzarella over the top of the pasta mixture and cook in the halogen oven at 250°C (480°F) for 3-4 minutes or until the cheese has melted. Serve with grated Parmesan.

pastrami & asparagus pasta

300 g (10 oz) dried penne pasta

125 g (4 oz) asparagus

125 g (4 oz) pastrami, chopped

100 g (3½ oz) sun-dried tomatoes in oil, drained and halved

1-2 teaspoons lemon juice (to taste)

salt and pepper

To serve

rocket leaves

50 g (2 oz) Parmesan cheese shavings

Cook the pasta according to the instructions on the packet. Drain thoroughly and set aside.

Meanwhile, trim the asparagus, cut the spears into shorter lengths and cook for 1-2 minutes in boiling water. Refresh under cold water and set aside.

Put the pasta in a casserole dish and add the pastrami, tomatoes and cooked asparagus. Add the lemon juice and season to taste with salt and pepper.

Gently toss everything together and cook on the lower rack of the halogen oven at 200°C (400°F) for 5 minutes to heat through. Serve the pasta in warm bowls with plenty of Parmesan shavings.

chorizo pasta bake

250 g (8 oz) fresh penne pasta

410 g (13¼ oz) can chopped tomatoes

125 g (4 oz) mozzarella, drained and chopped

100 g (3½ oz) chorizo, chopped

75 g (3 oz) large green olives, pitted

150 ml (¼ pint) boiling water

salt and pepper

50 g (2 oz) Parmesan cheese, grated, to serve

Put the pasta in a casserole dish and add the tomatoes, mozzarella, chorizo and olives. Season to taste with salt and pepper. Pour in the boiling water and mix everything together.

Cover with foil and cook on the lower rack of the halogen oven at 200°C (400°F) for 20 minutes or until the pasta is cooked through.

Spoon the pasta on to serving plates and serve with grated Parmesan.

baked gnocchi

2 tablespoons olive oil

250 g (8 oz) mushrooms, halved

500 g (1 lb) fresh gnocchi

350 g (11½ oz) ready-made spinach and ricotta pasta sauce

50 g (2 oz) Parmesan cheese, grated, to serve

Heat the oil in a frying pan and cook the mushrooms over a medium heat for 3-4 minutes or until golden.

Meanwhile, cook the gnocchi in salted, boiling water for 1-2 minutes. Drain.

Transfer the gnocchi to a casserole dish and gently stir in the mushrooms and pasta sauce.

Place the dish on the lower rack of the halogen oven and cook at 200°C (400°F) for 15 minutes, covering the top with foil if it looks as if it will burn.

Serve this dish as a starter or main course with plenty of grated Parmesan.

Serves **2** Preparation time **10 minutes** Cooking time **16-18 minutes**

french bread pizza

2 small, part-baked
baguettes

1 garlic clove, halved

6 tablespoons tomato purée

175 fl (6 fl oz) passata

toppings of your choice,
such as ham, salami, tuna,
olives, peppers, sliced
mushrooms and mozzarella

salad, to serve (optional)

Put the baguettes on a baking sheet and cook in the
halogen oven at 180°C (350°F) for 10 minutes or until
almost cooked.

Cut each baguette in half lengthways and rub with the
cut side of the garlic.

Spread each piece of bread with 1 tablespoon tomato
purée, followed by a couple of tablespoons of passata.
Add the topping of your choice.

Put the pizzas on a baking sheet and bake on the
lower rack of the halogen oven at 200°C (400°F) for
6-8 minutes or until the topping is cooked and golden.

Serve with a crisp green salad, if liked, or as an
accompaniment to other pasta dishes.

ham & tomato **wraps**

2 flour tortilla wraps

2 tablespoons tomato paste

200 g (7 oz) cherry tomatoes, halved

6 slices of Parma ham, roughly torn

handful of baby spinach leaves

125 g (4 oz) buffalo mozzarella cheese, drained and broken into pieces

olive oil, for drizzling

pinch of dried oregano

Put a tortilla wrap on a baking sheet and spread over 1 tablespoon tomato paste. Add half the tomatoes, 3 slices of ham, half the spinach leaves and half the mozzarella.

Drizzle a little olive oil over the tortilla and sprinkle with dried oregano. Repeat with the remaining ingredients to make a second wrap.

Cook the wraps on the lower rack of the halogen oven at 180°C (350°F) for 10–12 minutes.

Serve as a quick snack or as a starter with a small side salad.

Red Pepper Burgers (see page 59)

Cooking pies in a halogen oven

Steak & Kidney Pies (see page 62)

Honey & Sesame Salmon (see page 71)

goats' cheese pizza

1 thin and crispy pizza base

2 tablespoons ready-made onion relish

2 tomatoes, thinly sliced

50 g (2 oz) baby mushrooms, sliced

100 g (3½ oz) goats' cheese, thinly sliced

1 tablespoon ready-made green pesto

15 g (½ oz) wild rocket leaves, to garnish

Put the pizza base on a baking sheet. Spread the onion relish over the pizza.

Scatter the tomatoes and mushrooms over the top and add the slices of cheese.

Cook on the lower rack of the halogen oven at 180°C (350°F) for 8 minutes or until golden.

Drizzle some pesto over the top of the pizza and serve garnished with a handful of rocket leaves.

vegetarian dishes

vegetarian moussaka

500 g (1 lb) potatoes, cut into thick slices

1 aubergine, sliced

1 onion, chopped

2 garlic cloves, crushed

2 red peppers, cored, deseeded and sliced

2 tablespoons thyme or marjoram leaves

4 tablespoons olive oil

300 g (10 oz) cherry tomatoes

250 g (8 oz) passata

250 g (8 oz) feta cheese, sliced

300 ml (½ pint) natural yogurt

3 eggs

25 g (1 oz) Parmesan cheese, grated

To serve

Garlic Bread (see page 73)

green salad

Put the potatoes in a large saucepan of boiling water and cook for 5 minutes. Drain and arrange the potato slices on 2 baking sheets with the aubergine, onion, garlic and red peppers.

Sprinkle over the herbs, drizzle with oil and roast on the lower rack of the halogen oven at 200°C (400°F) for 20 minutes, turning halfway through the cooking time. Add the tomatoes after 15 minutes' cooking time.

Transfer half the vegetables to a casserole dish and spoon over half the passata and all the feta. Top with the remaining vegetables and passata.

Mix together the yogurt, eggs and Parmesan and pour over the vegetables. Cover the casserole dish with foil and cook on the lower rack at 200°C (400°F) for 20–25 minutes, removing the foil for the last 5 minutes to brown the top.

Serve the moussaka with chunks of warm garlic bread and a crisp green salad.

haloumi kebabs

50 g (2 oz) basil, plus extra
to serve

8 tablespoons olive oil

250 g (8 oz) haloumi
cheese, drained and cubed

1 large red pepper, cored,
deseeded and chopped

6 button mushrooms,
halved

1 courgette, roughly cubed

400 g (13 oz) spaghetti

2 tablespoons pine nuts

salt and pepper

Put the basil and oil in a small food processor or blender, season to taste with salt and pepper and process to a purée.

Transfer 2 tablespoons of the purée to a large bowl, add the haloumi, pepper, mushrooms and courgette and mix gently together.

Dry-fry the pine nuts in a nonstick frying pan over a medium heat for 4–5 minutes, stirring occasionally, until toasted. Set aside.

Thread the haloumi and vegetables alternately on to presoaked wooden skewers. Place them on the upper rack of the halogen oven and cook at 250°C (480°F) for 8–10 minutes or until the vegetables are tender.

Meanwhile, cook the spaghetti according to the instructions on the packet.

Drain the spaghetti well and toss with a couple of tablespoons of the remaining basil purée and the toasted pine nuts.

Transfer the spaghetti to 4 warm serving plates and arrange the kebabs on the top.

Serves **2** Preparation time **15 minutes** Cooking time **33–40 minutes**

baked butternut squash

1 butternut squash, about 25 cm (10 inches) long

3 tablespoons half-fat crème fraîche, plus extra to serve

1 teaspoon paprika, plus extra for sprinkling

3 spring onions, trimmed and finely chopped

2 tablespoons grated Parmesan cheese

2 tablespoons coarse breadcrumbs

Cut the squash in half lengthways. Use a spoon to scoop out and discard the seeds.

Transfer the squash to a casserole dish, put it on the lower rack of the halogen oven and cook at 250°C (480°F) for 25–30 minutes or until the flesh is soft.

Put the squash halves on a chopping board until they are cool enough to touch. Scrape the flesh into a bowl, leaving the skins intact.

Roughly mash the flesh with the crème fraîche, paprika and spring onions.

Transfer the mixture back into the skins and place them in the casserole dish. Sprinkle over the Parmesan and breadcrumbs.

Return the squash shells to the lower rack of the halogen oven and cook at 200°C (400°F) for a further 8–10 minutes or until the tops are brown.

Serve the squash in warm bowls with a sprinkling of paprika and a little crème fraîche on the side.

italian bean stew

3 tablespoons olive oil

4 celery sticks, sliced

4 carrots, sliced

3 leeks, sliced

2 garlic cloves, crushed

100 ml (3½ fl oz) white wine

2 x 400 g (13 oz) cans chopped tomatoes

grated rind and juice of 1 lemon

600 ml (1 pint) vegetable stock

410 g (13¼ oz) borlotti beans, rinsed and drained

410 g (13¼ oz) can cannellini beans, rinsed and drained

small handful of oregano

Heat the oil in a casserole dish over a medium heat. Add the celery and carrots and cook for 5–6 minutes. Add the leeks and cook for a further 3–4 minutes.

Stir in the garlic and wine. Bring the mixture to the boil and simmer until the liquid reduces.

Add the tomatoes and lemon rind and juice. Pour in the stock and transfer the casserole to the lower rack of the halogen oven. Cook, stirring occasionally, at 200°C (400°F) for 25–30 minutes or until the vegetables are just tender. The liquid should have reduced and thickened.

Stir in the beans and cook for a further 5 minutes. Serve in warm bowls garnished with a little oregano.

goats' cheese tarts

plain flour, for dusting

375g (12 oz) ready-rolled puff pastry

150 g (5 oz) goats' cheese, broken into pieces

250 g (8 oz) cherry tomatoes, halved

1 egg, beaten with a little water

4 slices of Parma ham (optional)

salt and pepper

To serve

rocket leaves

olive oil

large sprigs of basil

Dust your work surface with flour and unroll the pastry. Cut it into 4 pieces, each 8-10 cm (3-4 inches) square, and place them on a small, nonstick baking sheet.

Arrange the cheese and tomatoes in the centre of each of the pastry squares. Season to taste with salt and pepper and brush the edges with the beaten egg.

Place the baking sheet on the lower rack of the halogen oven and cook at 230°C (450°F) for 12-15 minutes or until the pastry has puffed and is golden.

Serve the tarts hot on a bed of rocket leaves, drizzled with some olive oil and garnished with a sprig of basil.

italian garlic potatoes

750 g (1½ lb) baby new potatoes

1 red pepper, cored, deseeded and chopped

1 yellow pepper, cored, deseeded and chopped

3 garlic cloves, chopped

low-fat oil spray

4 ripe tomatoes, chopped

250 g (8 oz) mozzarella cheese, drained and diced

20 g (¾ oz) basil leaves, torn

salt and pepper

Put the potatoes and red and yellow peppers in a roasting tin. Add the garlic, season to taste with salt and pepper and spray with oil.

Place the roasting tin on the lower rack of the halogen oven and cook at 250°C (480°F) for 40 minutes. Stir in the tomatoes and scatter over the mozzarella.

Cook for a further 5 minutes or until the mozzarella is melted. Sprinkle over the torn basil leaves and serve.

Serves 4 Preparation time **15 minutes plus chilling** Cooking time **5-10 minutes**

spiced veggie burgers

100 g (3½ oz) couscous

2 tablespoons olive oil

1 small onion, finely chopped

2 garlic cloves, finely chopped

1 red chilli, deseeded and finely chopped

1 teaspoon cumin seeds

½ teaspoon ground coriander

410 g (13¼ oz) can cannellini beans, rinsed and drained

2 tablespoons roughly chopped coriander leaves

grated rind of 1 lemon

1 egg, beaten

salt and pepper

To serve

crusty buns

green salad

sweet chilli sauce or ketchup

Cook the couscous according to the instructions on the packet.

Meanwhile, heat the oil in a frying pan and cook the onion, garlic and chilli over a medium heat for 4-5 minutes. Add the cumin seeds and coriander and cook for a further 1 minute.

Tip the beans into a large bowl and mash to form a coarse paste. Stir in the onion mixture, couscous, coriander leaves, lemon rind and beaten egg. Season to taste with salt and pepper.

Divide the mixture into 4 equal pieces and form each into a patty. Cover with foil and transfer to the refrigerator for a couple of hours.

Put the patties on a baking sheet and cook on the upper rack of the halogen oven at 200°C (400°F) for 5-10 minutes.

Serve the patties between split crusty buns with salad and sweet chilli sauce or ketchup.

vegetarian chilli

2 tablespoons olive oil

1 red pepper, cored, deseeded and chopped

1 yellow pepper, cored, deseeded and chopped

3 garlic cloves, chopped

2 teaspoons cumin seeds, lightly crushed

300 g (10 oz) frozen meat-free mince, such as Quorn

350 g (11½ oz) ready-made tomato pasta sauce

150 ml (¼ pint) water

410 g (13¼ oz) can kidney beans, rinsed and drained

1 tablespoon Worcestershire sauce

To serve

boiled rice

Garlic Bread (see page 73)

Heat the oil in a frying pan and cook the peppers over a medium heat for 5 minutes. Reduce the heat slightly and add the garlic, cumin seeds and vegetarian mince.

Transfer the mixture to a casserole dish. Mix in the tomato sauce, add the measured water to the jar, swirl it round and pour into the casserole. Stir in the kidney beans and add the Worcestershire sauce.

Cook on the lower rack of the halogen oven at 250°C (480°F) for 10–15 minutes or until the sauce is thick.

Serve with fluffy white rice and garlic bread.

dinner parties

italian halibut & prawns

4 halibut fillets, each 150–175 g (5-6 oz)

2 tablespoons olive oil

100 g (3½ oz) cooked, peeled prawns (thawed if frozen)

6 small sprigs of lemon thyme

Parmesan sauce

150 ml (¼ pint) double cream

6 tablespoons white wine

75 g (3 oz) Parmesan cheese, grated

Arrange the fish fillets on a baking sheet and drizzle over the olive oil.

Set the baking sheet on the upper rack of the halogen oven and cook the fish fillets at 250°C (480°F) for 3 minutes each side.

Add the prawns and 2 sprigs of lemon thyme and cook for a further 2 minutes, still at 250°C (480°F). Season to taste with salt and pepper.

Meanwhile, make the sauce. Put the cream in a saucepan and heat gently, whisking constantly. Add the wine and Parmesan and continue to cook, stirring, until melted and smooth.

Serve the fish with the prawns, pour the sauce on top and garnish with the remaining sprigs of lemon thyme.

beef wellington

1 kg (2 lb) beef fillet, trimmed

1 tablespoon chopped thyme leaves

2 tablespoons vegetable oil

2 tablespoons English mustard

250 g (8 oz) ready-made puff pastry (thawed if frozen)

1 egg, beaten

30 g (1¼ oz) butter

salt and pepper

Season the beef with salt and pepper and sprinkle with chopped thyme.

Heat a frying pan until it is very hot and add the oil. Cook the beef briefly, turning occasionally, until brown on all sides. Remove the beef from the pan, allow it to cool and spread mustard over the sides.

Roll out the pastry so that it is big enough to wrap around the beef. Place the beef in the centre, roll up the pastry to form a parcel and brush the edges with beaten egg, pressing them down to seal. Brush the outer surfaces of the pastry with beaten egg and transfer the parcel to the refrigerator for 30 minutes.

Put the pastry parcel on a piece of buttered baking parchment. Transfer to the lower rack of the halogen oven and bake at 160°C (325°F) for 30 minutes until the pastry is golden-brown and the beef is cooked to your liking; test it by inserting a skewer into the beef through the pastry. You may need to cover the pastry with foil for the first 15 minutes of cooking to prevent it from burning.

Remove the beef Wellington from the oven and allow it to rest for 5 minutes. Serve it sliced with vegetables of your choice.

sweet & sour meatballs

450 g (14½ oz) pork mince

1 small onion, finely chopped

1 garlic clove, crushed

low-fat oil spray

1 red pepper, cored, deseeded and diced

1 green pepper, cored, deseeded and diced

125 g (4 oz) mangetout

350 g (11½ oz) tomatoes, quartered

125 g (4 oz) can pineapple chunks in natural juice, drained

100 ml (3½ fl oz) pineapple juice

2 tablespoons soy sauce

2 tablespoons tomato purée

1 tablespoon white wine vinegar

1 teaspoon cornflour

pasta, to serve

Put the mince in a large bowl and add the onion and garlic. Mix thoroughly to combine and shape into 20 small balls.

Heat a large, nonstick frying pan and spray with oil. Quickly stir-fry the meatballs, a few at a time, to brown and seal them.

Transfer the meatballs to a casserole dish. Add the peppers, mangetout and tomatoes and cook on the lower rack of the halogen oven at 200°C (400°F) for 1-2 minutes.

Stir in the pineapple chunks and pineapple juice, soy sauce, tomato purée and vinegar and cook, still at 200°C (400°F), for 5-10 minutes or until bubbling. Reduce the heat, cover with foil and simmer for a further 10 minutes.

Mix the cornflour with a little cold water to make a thin paste. Mix this into the casserole and cook, stirring, until the sauce thickens a little.

Serve the meatballs and the sauce with pasta, such as tagliatelle.

Pastrami & Asparagus Pasta (see page 84)

Cooking a pizza in a halogen oven

Goats' Cheese Pizza (see page 93)

Summer Fruits Pudding (see page 140)

bacon & bruschetta

5 rashers of bacon

1 small onion, chopped

1 garlic clove, crushed

4 cherry tomatoes, chopped

½ baguette, cut into 2.5 cm (1 inch) slices

75 ml (3 fl oz) olive oil, plus extra to serve

50 g (2 oz) mature Cheddar cheese, grated

sprigs of parsley, to garnish

To serve

balsamic vinegar

side salad

Put the bacon in a small dish to collect the fat and cook on the lower rack of the halogen oven at 200°C (400°F) for 5 minutes or until crispy. Crumble the bacon rashers.

Heat the bacon fat in a nonstick frying pan over a medium heat and cook the onion, garlic and tomatoes until soft. Mix the bacon with the onion and tomatoes.

Brush the bread with oil, place on the upper rack of the halogen oven and cook at 220-230°C (425-450°F) until toasted. Keep an eye on it so that it doesn't burn.

Place a spoonful of the bacon mixture on top of the toast and sprinkle with grated cheese. Garnish with parsley sprigs.

Return the bruschetta to the halogen oven for a couple of minutes to melt the cheese.

Serve the bruschetta, drizzled with oil and balsamic vinegar, as a starter with a small side salad.

garlicky roast beef

2 tablespoons olive oil

3 garlic cloves, crushed

225 g (7½ oz) breadcrumbs

30 g (1¼ oz) chopped parsley

½ teaspoon salt

½ teaspoon black pepper

1.5 kg (3 lb) beef joint

To serve

Roast Potatoes (see page 124)

seasonal vegetables

Heat the oil in a frying pan, add the garlic and cook for 2 minutes, pressing the juice from the garlic into the oil. Add the breadcrumbs, parsley, salt and pepper and mix together.

Pat the meat dry with kitchen paper. Press the breadcrumb mixture on to the joint, coating well.

Put the joint on the lower rack of the halogen oven, cover it with a piece of foil and cook at 200°C (400°F) for 35–40 minutes, removing the foil for the last 5 minutes to give a crisp crust.

Remove the meat from oven and allow to stand for 15–20 minutes before carving.

Serve with roast potatoes and seasonal vegetables.

Serves **2**   Preparation time **15 minutes plus chilling**   Cooking time **10–15 minutes**

peppercorn steak

2 rump or sirloin steaks, each about 450 g (14½ oz) and 4 cm (1¾ inch) thick

1 tablespoon white peppercorns, crushed

1 tablespoon black peppercorns, crushed

Chunky Chips (see page 123), to serve

Peppercorn sauce

½ tablespoon olive oil

50 g (2 oz) unsalted butter

2 shallots, finely diced

2 tablespoons Worcestershire sauce

2 tablespoons brandy

100 ml (3½ fl oz) beef stock

1 teaspoon green peppercorns

1 teaspoon Dijon mustard

3 tablespoons double cream

salt

Dry the steaks with kitchen paper and press the black and white peppercorns into both sides. Cover with foil or clingfilm and transfer to the refrigerator for 2-3 hours.

Put the steak on the lower rack of the halogen oven and cook at 200°C (400°F) for 5-10 minutes.

Meanwhile, make the sauce. Heat the oil and butter in a frying pan and cook the shallots over a medium heat until soft but not brown.

Add the Worcestershire sauce, brandy and stock to the frying pan. Cook rapidly, scraping the bottom of the pan to incorporate the flavours. Add the green peppercorns, mustard and cream. Season to taste with salt.

Remove the meat from the oven and slice it diagonally. Add the meat to the sauce. Stir to combine the meat juices with the pepper sauce and to warm the meat through. Serve with homemade chips.

Serves **2**   Preparation time **10 minutes**   Cooking time **15–20 minutes**

balsamic-glazed salmon

low-fat oil spray

2 garlic cloves, minced

1 tablespoon white wine

1 tablespoon honey

1 tablespoon balsamic vinegar

1 teaspoon Dijon mustard

2 salmon fillets, each about 150 g (5 oz)

1 teaspoon chopped oregano

salt and pepper

To serve

green salad

new potatoes

Line a small baking sheet with foil and spray with oil.

In a frying pan dry-fry the garlic, stirring, over a medium heat until soft. Mix in the wine, honey, balsamic vinegar and mustard. Season to taste with salt and pepper. Simmer, uncovered, for about 3 minutes or until slightly thickened.

Arrange the salmon on the foil-lined baking sheet. Brush the fish with the balsamic glaze and sprinkle over the oregano.

Put the salmon on the upper rack of the halogen oven and cook at 250°C (480°F) for 10-14 minutes or until the flesh flakes easily with a fork.

Brush the fillets with the remaining glaze and season with salt and pepper. Serve the fillets with a green salad and new potatoes.

prawn skewers

3 lemons, cut into wedges

3 limes, cut into wedges

18 large cooked, peeled prawns

rocket salad, to serve

Sweet chilli dip

2 tablespoons clear honey

1 teaspoon Dijon mustard

1 pinch of dried red chilli flakes, crushed

Thread the lemon and lime wedges and prawns alternately on to 6 presoaked wooden skewers.

Make the dip. In a bowl mix together the honey, mustard and dried chillies and spoon or brush the mixture over the skewers.

Place the skewers on the upper rack of the halogen oven and cook at 250°C (480°F) for 2-3 minutes on each side until the glaze is sticky and the lemon and limes are beginning to blacken around the edges.

Serve the skewers straight from the oven on a bed of rocket salad.

Serves **2**   Preparation time **5 minutes**   Cooking time **21-22 minutes**

mozzarella chicken

2 boneless, skinless chicken
breasts, each about
125 g (4 oz)

2 teaspoons pesto

125 g (4 oz) mozzarella
cheese, drained and sliced

Mediterranean Vegetables
(see page 128), to serve

Put the chicken breasts in a plastic bag and hit them
a few times with a rolling pin to flatten them.

Place the chicken breasts on the lower rack of
the halogen oven and cook at 200°C (400°F) for
18 minutes, covering them with foil if necessary so
that the tops don't burn.

Remove the chicken from the oven, spread with pesto
and add some sliced mozzarella.

Return the chicken to the halogen oven and cook for
a further 3-4 minutes until the cheese has melted.

Serve immediately with Mediterranean vegetables.

Serves **2**   Preparation time **10 minutes**   Cooking time **12–15 minutes**

herby baked halibut

1½ teaspoons chopped rosemary

pinch of pepper

1 garlic clove, minced

2 tablespoons seasoned breadcrumbs

2 halibut steaks, each about 150 g (5 oz)

1 teaspoon olive oil

salt

To serve

new potatoes

mangetout

In a bowl mix together the rosemary, pepper, garlic and seasoned breadcrumbs. Mash to a paste with a fork or in food processor.

Season both sides of the halibut with salt and put the fish in a lightly oiled baking dish. Brush the fish with oil and press half the breadcrumb mixture on top of each steak.

Place the baking dish on the upper rack of the halogen oven and cook at 250°C (480°F) for 12–15 minutes or until fish is flaky.

Serve with new potatoes and mangetout.

side dishes

Serves 4   Preparation time **10 minutes**   Cooking time **40–45 minutes**

dauphinoise potatoes

1 kg (2 lb) Maris Piper potatoes, thinly sliced

25 g (1 oz) butter, plus extra for greasing

1 onion, sliced

2 garlic cloves, sliced

275 ml (9 fl oz) double cream

75 ml (3 fl oz) milk

salt and pepper

Layer the potatoes in a lightly buttered casserole dish. Add the onion and garlic to the dish and season to taste with salt and pepper.

Mix together the cream and milk and pour over the potatoes. Dot with butter.

Cover the dish with foil and cook on the lower rack of the halogen oven at 200°C (400°F) for 40–45 minutes, removing the foil after the first 25 minutes.

Serves 1   Preparation time **5 minutes**   Cooking time **45–50 minutes**

baked potatoes

1 large potato, such as King Edward

butter

salt

Wash the potato and while it is still damp sprinkle it with salt and prick the skin with a fork.

Put the potato on the lower rack of the halogen oven and cook at 200°C (400°F) for 45–50 minutes.

Cut the potato open and serve with a large knob of butter.

Serves **4**   Preparation time **5 minutes**   Cooking time **20-30 minutes**

chunky chips

875 g (1¾ lb) potatoes, such as Maris Piper or King Edward, quartered

2 tablespoons sunflower oil

sea salt

Put the potatoes in cold water to soak for 10 minutes. Drain and pat dry with kitchen paper.

Place the potatoes in a large bowl. Add the oil and turn the potatoes to coat thoroughly.

Transfer the potatoes to a shallow roasting tin or casserole dish and cook on the lower rack of the halogen oven at 250°C (480°F) for 20-30 minutes until golden-brown and cooked through. Sprinkle with sea salt and serve.

Serves **4**   Preparation time **5 minutes**   Cooking time **10-15 minutes**

sweet potato wedges

2 sweet potatoes, each cut into 12 wedges

4 tablespoons olive oil

1 teaspoon chilli flakes

sea salt and pepper

Put the potato wedges in a bowl, pour over the oil and turn to cover evenly. Add the chilli flakes and stir to combine. Season to taste with salt and pepper.

Place the potato wedges on the foil-covered lower rack of the halogen oven and cook at 250°C (480°F) for 10-15 minutes or until the potatoes are tender and golden-brown. Sprinkle with sea salt to serve.

Serves 4   Preparation time **10 minutes**   Cooking time **50 minutes**

roast potatoes

1 kg (2 lb) potatoes, halved

6 tablespoons olive oil

salt

Half-fill a large saucepan with cold water. Put the potatoes in the pan, add a pinch of salt and cover. As soon as the water boils, reduce the heat and cook for 6 minutes.

Drain the potatoes and shake them in a colander to roughen the edges.

Pour the oil into a roasting tin and place in the halogen oven at 250°C (480°F) for 5 minutes.

Put the potatoes into the hot fat and sprinkle with salt. Place on the lower rack of the halogen oven and cook, still at 250°C (480°F), for 25 minutes. Carefully turn them over and cook for another 25 minutes. Check that the potatoes don't burn, covering them with foil if necessary.

Serves **2**   Preparation time **5 minutes**   Cooking time **30 minutes**

parmesan potatoes

6 potatoes, such as Maris
Piper or King Edward

olive oil

50 g (2 oz) Parmesan
cheese, grated

sea salt

Scrub but do not peel potatoes. Cut them into 4 large chunks, put them in a bowl and add oil and salt to taste. Mix together to coat evenly.

Place the potatoes on the lower rack of the halogen oven and cook at 250°C (480°F) for 25 minutes, covering them with foil for the first 10 minutes so they do not burn. Sprinkle with Parmesan cheese and cook for a further 5 minutes.

Serves **4**   Preparation time **10 minutes**   Cooking time **35-45 minutes**

pilau rice

50 g (2 oz) butter

1 onion, chopped

225 g (7½ oz) basmati rice

1 bay leaf

3 cloves

5 cm (2 inch) cinnamon
stick

50 g (2 oz) flaked almonds

25 g (1 oz) raisins

600 ml (1 pint) water

Heat the butter in a frying pan and cook the onion over a medium heat until soft.

Transfer the onion to a casserole dish and add all the remaining ingredients. Mix well to combine.

Put the casserole in the halogen oven and cook at 250°C (480°F) until boiling. Reduce the temperature to 200°C (400°F), cover the dish with foil and simmer gently for 20-25 minutes or until all the water has been absorbed.

Drain the rice in a colander if necessary, fluff it up with a fork and serve immediately.

milk loaf

1½ teaspoon fresh yeast, crumbled

350 ml (12 fl oz) whole milk, at room temperature, plus extra for brushing

20 g (¾ oz) golden or maple syrup

250 g (8 oz) plain white flour, plus extra for dusting

250 g (8 oz) strong white flour

1¼ teaspoon fine sea salt

25 g (1 oz) unsalted butter, melted and cooled slightly

olive oil, for greasing

Put the yeast, milk and syrup in a large mixing bowl and whisk together. Add the flours and salt and mix with your hands to form a soft, sticky dough.

Pour over the still warm butter and mix this into the dough with your hands. Cover the bowl with clingfilm or a clean tea towel and leave to stand in a warm place for about 10 minutes.

Grease your hands and a flat surface with olive oil. Remove the dough from the bowl and knead it for 10 seconds. Form the dough into a round ball.

Wipe the bowl clean, grease it with a little oil and return the dough ball to the bowl. Leave to prove for a further 10 minutes.

Grease a loaf tin and dust it with flour. Divide the dough into 2 equal pieces, shape them into balls and place them in the loaf tin. Cover with a cloth and leave to rise for about 1½ hours or until almost doubled in height.

Brush the top of the loaf with some milk and cook in the halogen oven at 200°C (400°F) for 15 minutes. Reduce the heat to 180°C (350°F) and bake for another 25-30 minutes or until the top of the loaf is dark brown and the loaf has come away from the sides of the tin. You may need to cover the loaf with foil for the first 15 minutes to make sure it doesn't burn.

Serves **6**   Preparation time **15 minutes**   Cooking time **20 minutes**

cauliflower cheese

1 large cauliflower

500 ml (17 fl oz) full-cream milk

1 small onion, finely chopped

30 g (1¼ oz) butter

30 g (1¼ oz) plain flour

4 tablespoons double cream

3 tablespoons grated mature Cheddar cheese

salt and pepper

Break the cauliflower head into large florets.

Put the milk and onion into a pan and cook, stirring, over a medium heat. Bring to the boil, then set aside.

In another pan melt the butter over a low heat. Stir in the flour and cook for 30 seconds. Gradually add the hot milk and onion and bring to the boil, stirring until thickened. Remove the pan from the heat, stir in the cream and season to taste with salt and pepper.

Cook the cauliflower in a pan of boiling water for 4 minutes or until tender.

Drain the cauliflower and transfer to a casserole dish. Pour over the sauce, sprinkle with the cheese, then place the dish on the lower rack of the halogen oven and cook at 250°C (480°F) for 5 minutes or until the cauliflower is lightly golden.

Serves 4   Preparation time **10 minutes plus soaking**   Cooking time **20-25 minutes**

corn on the cob

4 corn cobs

125 g (4 oz) butter, softened

1 red chilli, deseeded and finely chopped

handful of chopped coriander leaves

Soak the corn in a bowl of cold water for 30 minutes.

In a bowl beat together the butter, chilli and coriander.

Cut 4 squares of foil, each large enough to enclose a cob, and place a cob on each piece. Spoon over the flavoured butter and wrap up the corn in the foil.

Cook on the lower rack of the halogen oven at 200°C (400°F) for 20-25 minutes. Unwrap the foil carefully, retaining the butter to serve with the corn.

Serves 2   Preparation time **10 minutes**   Cooking time **25 minutes**

mediterranean vegetables

2 courgettes, sliced

2 red onions, sliced

1 red pepper, cored, deseeded and cut into 2.5 cm (1 inch) pieces

1 orange pepper, cored, deseeded and cut into 2.5 cm (1 inch) pieces

1 garlic clove, finely chopped

3 tablespoons olive oil

2 teaspoons mixed dried herbs

Put the courgettes and onions in a casserole dish. Add the peppers and garlic.

Pour the oil over the vegetables, sprinkle with the herbs and toss gently to combine.

Put the casserole dish on the upper rack of the halogen oven and cook at 250°C (480°F) for 25 minutes.

Serves **2** Preparation time **10 minutes** Cooking time **20–25 minutes**

stuffed peppers

150 g (5 oz) couscous

2 red peppers

1 red onion, finely chopped

Prepare the couscous according to the instructions on the packet.

Meanwhile, cut the tops off the red peppers and core and deseed them.

Mix the onion with the couscous. Fill the peppers with couscous and place them on a baking sheet.

Cook the peppers on the lower rack of the halogen oven at 250°C (480°F) for 20–25 minutes.

Serves **6** Preparation time **10 minutes** Cooking time **45 minutes**

ratatouille

4 tablespoons olive oil

3 garlic cloves, roughly chopped

1 kg (2 lb) tomatoes, roughly chopped

2 red onions, cubed

3 red peppers, cored, deseeded and cubed

2 aubergines, cubed

4 courgettes, cubed

salt and pepper

chopped herbs, to serve

Put the oil, garlic and vegetables in a casserole dish. Mix them together and season to taste with salt and pepper.

Put the casserole in the halogen oven and cook at 200°C (400°F) for 45 minutes or until the vegetables are tender.

To serve, finish with a dash of oil and a sprinkling of herbs of your choice.

side dishes **129**

desserts

yorkshire curd tarts

175 g (6 oz) ready-made shortcrust pastry (thawed if frozen)

vegetable oil, for greasing

125 g (4 oz) low-fat cottage cheese

finely grated rind of 1 lemon

25 g (1 oz) sultanas

25 g (1 oz) demerara sugar

pinch of ground nutmeg

1 egg

Roll out the pastry and use a biscuit cutter to cut out 12 circles, each about 10 cm (4 inches) across. Put them in a lightly greased 12-hole baking tin.

Push the cottage cheese through a sieve into a bowl. Add the lemon rind, sultanas, sugar, nutmeg and egg and beat together.

Spoon the filling into the pastry cases and bake on the upper rack of the halogen oven at 180°C (350°F) for 10-15 minutes until the filling is just set to the touch.

Remove the tarts from the oven and leave to cool on a metal cake rack before serving.

oaty crumbles

75 g (3 oz) plain white flour

75 g (3 oz) demerara sugar

75 g (3 oz) porridge oats

½ teaspoon ground nutmeg

75 g (3 oz) margarine

1 tablespoon clear honey

Line 2 baking sheets with nonstick baking parchment.

In a bowl mix together the flour, sugar, porridge oats and nutmeg.

Melt the margarine in a small saucepan, stir in the honey and pour the mixture over the dry ingredients. Mix well and place 16 spoonfuls of the mixture, set well apart, on the prepared baking sheet.

Place the baking sheet on the lower rack of the halogen oven and bake at 180°C (350°F) for 15 minutes or until the biscuits have spread out and are golden-brown. Cover them with foil for the first 7-8 minutes of the cooking time so they do not burn.

Remove the biscuits from the oven and leave to cool on a metal cake rack before serving.

vanilla melts

100 g (3 oz) margarine

50 g (2 oz) icing sugar

½ vanilla pod

75 g (3 oz) self-raising flour

75 g (3 oz) cornflour

Line 2 baking sheets with nonstick baking parchment.

Put the margarine in a warm mixing bowl and sift in the icing sugar. Cream together to make a pale, fluffy mixture.

Use a small, sharp knife to slice the vanilla pod in half lengthways. Scoop out the tiny black seeds and beat them into the creamed mixture. Add the flour and cornflour and mix to form a stiff dough.

Form the dough into 16 small balls and arrange them well apart on the baking sheets, pressing them down with a fork.

Cover the balls with foil and cook in the halogen oven at 180°C (350°F) for 12–15 minutes until just golden. Remove the foil for the last couple of minutes to brown the tops of the biscuits.

raisin & honey flapjacks

125 g (4 oz) margarine

125 g (4 oz) demerara sugar

3 tablespoons clear honey

50 g (2 oz) raisins

1 teaspoon ground mixed spice

200 g (7 oz) rolled oats

Line a 25-30 cm (10-12 inch) square baking tin with nonstick baking parchment.

Put the margarine, sugar and honey in a small saucepan and heat gently until dissolved. Stir in the raisins, mixed spice and rolled oats.

Press the mixture into the prepared tin and level with the back of a metal spoon.

Cover the tin with foil and cook the biscuits on the lower rack of the halogen oven at 180°C (350°F) for 20 minutes. Mark out pieces while the flapjack is still warm.

apple & cinnamon ring

low-fat oil spray

150 g (5 oz) self-raising flour

1 teaspoon baking powder

½ teaspoon ground cinnamon

350 g (12 oz) cooking apples, peeled, cored and coarsely grated

2 tablespoons lemon juice

50 g (2 oz) demerara sugar

50 g (2 oz) sultanas

50 ml (2 fl oz) sunflower oil

2 eggs

100 ml (3½ fl oz) skimmed milk

2 tablespoons reduced-sugar apricot jam

whipped double cream, to serve

Spray a small ring mould with oil.

Sift the flour, baking powder and cinnamon into a mixing bowl. Mix the grated apple with the lemon juice and stir into the flour with the sugar and sultanas.

In a bowl beat together the oil, eggs, milk and jam. Make a well in the centre of the dry ingredients and pour in the milk and egg mixture. Mix together.

Spoon the mixture into the prepared mould and level the surface.

Cover with foil and cook on the lower rack of the halogen oven at 180°C (350°F) for 35-40 minutes. Check that the mixture is cooked through by inserting a skewer into the cake; if it comes out clean the cake is ready.

Allow the cake to cool in the tin for 10 minutes, then loosen the edges with a palette knife. Cut into 10 slices and serve warm with whipped double cream.

brownie pudding

120 g (3¾ oz) unsalted butter, plus extra for greasing

4 large eggs, at room temperature

400 g (13 oz) sugar

120 g (3¾ oz) cocoa powder

65 g (2½ oz) plain flour

1 vanilla pod

whipped double cream, to serve

Lightly butter a casserole dish. Melt the remaining butter and set aside.

Beat together the eggs and sugar until thick and pale yellow. In a separate bowl sift together the cocoa powder and flour.

Use a small, sharp knife to slice the vanilla pod in half lengthways. Scoop out the tiny black seeds and add them to the flour and cocoa powder. Stir to combine. Slowly pour in the cooled butter, mix again and combine with the egg and sugar mixture.

Pour the mixture into the casserole dish and place it in a larger dish half-filled with hot water.

Cover the dish with foil and cook the pudding on the lower rack of the halogen oven at 180°C (350°F) for 40 minutes, removing the foil for the last 10 minutes to brown the top. The centre of cake is supposed to look undercooked and sticky. Serve with whipped double cream.

jamaican crumble

2 tablespoons lemon juice

4 teaspoons soft brown sugar

6 tablespoons water

250 g (8 oz) fresh pineapple, cubed

8 lychees, stoned and halved

4 dates, stoned and halved

½ banana, sliced

vanilla ice cream, to serve

Crumble

2 oz (50 g) wholemeal or plain flour

30 g (1¼ oz) margarine, chilled

½ oz (15 g) porridge oats

pinch of ground ginger

2 teaspoons soft brown sugar

4 teaspoons desiccated coconut

Make the crumble. Put the flour in a bowl and add the margarine. Rub together with your fingertips until the mixture resembles breadcrumbs. Stir in the porridge oats, ginger, sugar and coconut.

In a small saucepan stir together the lemon juice, sugar and water over a low heat until the sugar dissolves.

Mix together the prepared fruit in a casserole dish, pour over the syrup and sprinkle the crumble topping evenly over the fruit.

Cover the dish with foil and bake on the lower rack of the halogen oven at 200°C (400°F) for 20–30 minutes, removing the foil for the last 5 minutes.

Serve hot with vanilla ice cream.

treacle **pudding**

100 g (3½ oz) butter, plus extra for greasing

6 large tablespoons golden syrup

100 g (3½ oz) caster sugar

2 eggs

½ teaspoon vanilla extract

100 g (3½ oz) self-raising flour

custard, to serve

Butter a small baking dish. Put the syrup in the bottom.

Put the butter and sugar in a blender or food processor and mix until pale. Beat in the eggs one by one, then add the vanilla extract. Add the flour and combine until just mixed.

Scrape the mixture into the dish on top of the syrup and cook on the lower rack of the halogen oven at 220°C (425°F) for 20 minutes or until the pudding is risen and golden.

Serve hot with custard.

Serves **4-6** Preparation time **15 minutes** Cooking time **30-35 minutes**

summer fruits pudding

350 g (11½ oz) summer fruits (thawed if frozen)

3 tablespoons light muscovado sugar

4 tablespoons blueberry jam

6 medium-sized ripe pears, peeled, cored and quartered

50 g (2 oz) fresh white breadcrumbs

25 g (1 oz) butter, melted

cream, to serve

Put the summer fruits in a large bowl and mix with the sugar and jam. Add the pears and toss to mix.

Tip the fruit into a deep baking dish. Cover with foil and cook on the lower rack of the halogen oven at 250°C (480°F) for 20 minutes. Insert a skewer to check if the pears are tender; if not, return the dish to the oven for another 5 minutes or until the pears feel soft.

Mix the breadcrumbs with the butter and scatter over the fruit. Bake uncovered in the oven at 200°C (400°F) for 10 minutes or until the topping is golden and crispy. Serve with cream.

Serves 2   Preparation time **10 minutes**   Cooking time **15 minutes**

baked bananas

3 bananas, cut into chunks

25 g (1 oz) butter

50 g (2 oz) soft brown sugar

grated rind and juice of 1 lemon

grated rind and juice of 1 orange

2-3 tablespoons rum (optional)

vanilla ice cream, to serve

Arrange the banana pieces in a small casserole dish and dot with the butter. Sprinkle over the sugar and lemon and orange rind.

Mix together the fruit juices and rum, if using, and pour over the bananas.

Cover the bananas with foil and cook on the lower rack of the halogen oven at 220°C (425°F) for 15 minutes or until they are piping hot. Serve immediately with vanilla ice cream.

index

acknowledgements

With thanks to JML (www.JMLdirect.com) for lending us their halogen ovens for the photoshoot.

Executive Editor Eleanor Maxfield
Managing Editor Clare Churly
Creative Director Tracy Killick
Designer Janis Utton
Photographer Ian Garlick
Food Stylist Eliza Baird
Stylist Sarah Waller
Senior Production Controller Amanda Mackie